A CENTURY OF CUBAN WRITERS

IN FLORIDA

A Century of Cuban Writers in Florida

Selected Prose and Poetry

Edited with an Introduction by
Carolina Hospital and
Jorge Cantera

PINEAPPLE PRESS, INC.

Sarasota, Florida

ɔk *was made possible in part by*
t for Cuban-American Studies,
a project of the Cuban-American National Foundation.

Inquiries should be addressed to:
Pineapple Press, Inc.
P.O. Box 3899
Sarasota, Florida 34230

Library of Congress Cataloging in Publication Data

Acentury of Cuban writers in Florida : selected prose and poetry / edited with an introduction by Carolina Hospital and Jorge Cantera.
    P.   Cm.
    Includes bibliographical references (p.   ) and index.
    ISBN 1-56164-104-9 (pbk. : alk. Paper)
    1. Amercian literature—Cuban American authors. 2. Cuban American literature (Spanish)—Translations into English. 3. Cuban Americans—Florida—Literary collections. 4. American literature—Florida. I. Hospital, Carolina, 1957– . II. Cantera, Jorge, 1960– .
PS508.C83C46 1996   96-20647
810.8'8687291—dc20   CIP

First Edition
10 9 8 7 6 5 4 3 2 1

Design by Carol Tornatore
Printed and bound by Edwards Brothers, Ann Arbor, Michigan

*This book is dedicated to Felix Varela
and the spirit of education, tolerance,
and sacrifice he embodied.*

CONTENTS

CONTENTS

CONTENTS

PREFACE

$\mathcal{K}$*ey West*, Tampa, and Miami would hardly be recognizable today to a resident from the early nineteenth century. For instance, Key West then was an isolated town with a couple of hotels, several boardinghouses, and neat and attractive wooden homes on dusty roads. Tampa looked similar. Miami was even sparser until the end of the century. "Sleepy towns," some may have called them, yet hardly so. For particularly in Key West and Tampa, bustling cloisters of Cuban exiles were developing active communities. By the time the young Cuban poet Juana Borrero arrived in Key West in 1896, the island's population had increased to over twelve thousand, with Cubans constituting the majority. They were involved in Cuban as well as local politics, revolutionary activism against the Spanish crown, espionage, a growing local economy, journalism, and, most importantly for their cultural legacy, literature.

All these activities were interrelated. The economies of both Key West and Ybor City grew rapidly in the nineteenth century after the development of the cigar industry, which was owned and worked by Cuban émigrés. The workers used their wages not only to increase the economic base of the cities, but also to fund pro-independence activities in Cuba.

These cigar workers also donated a part of their wages to hire *lectores,* readers who would entertain and educate them by reading from literary classics as well as newspapers. The *lectores* usually were prestigious literary figures from Cuba who had been forced into exile, such as Bonifacio Byrne. Reading at these cigar factories became their main source of livelihood. Furthermore, they would often use their position to promote both local and Cuban politics among the workers.

For more than a century, Cubans have established strong ties with Florida. They have left their mark in towns like St. Augustine, Key West, and Tampa; the latter two cities even had Cuban mayors in the nineteenth century. They continue to exert influence today in Miami and Tallahassee, as well as in other cities throughout Florida and the United States.

Many Cubans became permanent residents; others traveled back and forth between the island and Florida. The writers were no exception. For more than a century, Cuban writers have traveled to Florida to seek political asylum. Because of the long-standing contacts between the two places, Florida was seen as a natural refuge. Most of the writers who came before the 1950s returned to Cuba, except for a few, such as Felix Varela and Juana Borrero, who died in Florida. Those who arrived in Florida in the second half of the twentieth century have remained. As Felix Varela so well illustrates, most have shown love for both the home of their birth and their adopted land.

In spite of the close contacts between these two cultures and the participation of important Cuban figures in Florida's cultural and political history, the Cuban presence in Florida has been practically ignored in the study of Florida history, as well as U.S. history in general. Unless their specific focus concerns Hispanics in Florida, few books on Florida history include more than a slight mention or quick overview of Hispanics. This despite the fact that, for example, in 1891, Cubans in Key West alone numbered eight thousand — a majority of the small island's population and a third of the entire Cuban population in the U.S. At the end of the century, Cubans dominated the economy and culture of Key West, Ybor City, and West Tampa.

Even fewer books discuss the presence of Cuban writers. Many wrote in both languages or translated newspapers, textbooks, and popular novels into Spanish. They served and continue to serve as an important link between the two linguistic communities.

Many Floridians speak with pride of the fact that such literary figures as Robert Frost and Zora Neale Hurston lived in south Florida. Yet how many people realize that poet José Martí, leader of Cuba's independence movement, spent fifteen years of exile in New York? That during that time he made repeated and extensive visits to Tampa, Key West, Jacksonville, St. Petersburg, and Ocala? And that throughout these cities he gave public speeches to audiences of over five thousand people at a time?

How many realize that Cuban priest Felix Varela, one of the most important Latin American philosophers and educators of the nineteenth century, who spent thirty years in New York tending to poor Irish parishioners, was raised in St. Augustine, Florida, and spent his last years there, loved and admired by the locals?

How many realize that poet Heberto Padilla, who defected in 1980 after a controversial arrest which elicited the reaction of the European intellectual community, first resided in Florida in the early 1950s during the Batista regime and now lives in Miami Lakes?

These are only a few of the discoveries we made in our search for Cuban writers in Florida. We discovered more than we had anticipated. Our realization of this broad neglect of the Cuban presence in Florida history is what prompted us to include an extensive introduction to this anthology that would situate the Cuban exile writers within a broader historical frame.

We believe it is important to realize that the present communities of Cubans in Florida date back to a much earlier time. They are not just a current ethnic phenomenon. Cubans have participated in developing Florida's cultural, economic, and political history since its inception and therefore can lay claim to its heritage.

The purpose of our introductory essay is to trace the relationship of Cuba with Florida throughout more than a century and offer a description of the communities Cuban writers would have encountered in their stay in Florida. With the literary selections in the anthology, we hope to introduce students, scholars, and general readers to important Cuban literary figures who lived part of their lives in Florida. Because most of these writers are unknown to the majority of the non-Spanish-speaking community, including Cuban-Americans schooled in the United States, we have chosen to include some selections from these authors' major works, even though they may not have been written while living in Florida. It is often the case that authors do not even write about their daily experience in a place until years later when they no longer live there.

Many of the Cuban writers did contribute, however, to local newspapers and magazines while living in Florida, and, even though the presence of these newspapers and magazines is important to the everyday existence of these communities, we have chosen not to always include samples of these if the author is well known for other more significant texts. Nevertheless, because we recognize the importance of these newspapers and magazines to the everyday reality of these communities, we have mentioned them in the introduction. In addition, we have chosen some less familiar works by younger writers who are in the process of contributing to the Cuba-Florida axis.

We consider the collective presence of these writers in Florida the most important contribution to creating a consciousness that embraces the two geographical spaces. Our objective here is not to find every piece of writing written or published in Florida by Cubans (a goal not without merit for a different project) but, instead, to show that the current links between these two cultures are not an accident of history but a phenomenon grounded in historical precedent. The collective consciousness of these Cuban writers residing in Florida manifests this reality. Florida history, as well as Cuban history, is forever marked by this relationship.

We also believe that this anthology has value in introducing major Cuban writers and their major texts to the reader. The anthology is in English in order to reach a non-Spanish-speaking audience who may or may not have a Hispanic ancestry. It amazed us to find that, in spite of the close relationship shared by Cuba and Florida for centuries, few works by Cuban authors had been translated into English. By offering these works in English, we hope to open a window to a world previously inaccessible to many. We cannot underestimate the longevity and significance of the contact between the two cultures.

We acknowledge the help of numerous individuals who assisted in making these translations possible, in particular: Pablo Medina, David Miller, Ramón Bayardo Rancaño, and María Elena Valdés.

We regret that, due to space constraints or the inaccessibility of materials, we were unable to include samples from all the Cuban writers who have lived in Florida. Nevertheless, we have attempted to be as comprehensive as possible in the introduction, and we offer the selections here as the beginning of a journey and not an end. Finally, we also acknowledge the assistance of the Endowment for Cuban-American Studies, a project of the Cuban-American National Foundation, for helping to finance a portion of the research and translations necessary to complete this work.

To all the writers and friends who encouraged us along the way, and especially to Carlos Medina for his suggestions and contributions in editing the manuscript, thanks so much for your patience and support.

Carolina Hospital

INTRODUCTION

FLORIDA AND CUBA: TIES THAT BIND

Jorge Cantera
Carolina Hospital

*B*efore Columbus even dreamed of sailing west, Arawak Indians from Cuba would regularly make dangerous trips across the Florida straits. Their goal was trade and commerce with south Florida's Tequesta Indians. When the Europeans arrived in the Americas in 1492, the contact between these two geographic locations continued, for Cuba became a major staging area for the Spanish conquest of the new territories, including Florida. As Florida's history developed, and its relationship with Cuba continued, the history of these two communities became intertwined.

The first known Cubans of European descent to come to Florida's shore arrived in 1538, in the company of Hernando de Soto, when he sailed from Cuba to explore Florida. Their names were Diego De Oliva, Goméz Suárez de Figueroa, and Pedro Morón. These men, however, were not writers; they served De Soto's expedition as scouts, porters, and interpreters. Very little is known about these early Cuban explorers, except that they were of mixed ancestry, being the offspring of Spanish *conquistadores* and island natives.

The contact between Florida and Cuba manifested itself in diverse realms, such as trade, conquest, exploration, industry, refuge or exile, and multicultural exchange. Nevertheless, the constant thread throughout these endeavors and throughout the ages has been held by the men and women of letters. For chroniclers, historians, philosophers, journalists, agitators, political essayists, novelists, and poets have been the mile markers of cultural ties between Florida and Cuba, a symbiotic relationship that extends from the sixteenth century to the present. Even though the anthology includes selections only from major Cuban literary figures from the nineteenth and twentieth centuries, this general introduction will present a broader historical context of the events, individuals, and communities that served as a stage. Individualized introductions providing more specific literary and biographical data on each author will precede every selection.

The earliest literary contacts between Cuba and Florida were made when the first Cuban writers of European descent began arriving in Florida. These writers were the early chronicle writers, missionaries, and scholars who made their way to Spanish Florida and began recording the early history of Spanish Florida and its native American population.

Among the earliest and most distinguished Cuban-born Florida missionaries during this early period were Friars Luis Sánchez and Tiburcio De Osorio. Friar Sánchez was killed by the Joruro Indians at the Mission of Mayaca in 1696, while Friar De Osorio died at the Patali mission near present-day Tallahassee in 1704 when a British column under the command of British Carolina Governor James Moore attacked and destroyed the Spanish missions in Georgia and northern Florida. Two other well-known Cuban-born missionaries were Friars Antonio De Florencia and Francisco Marrón. De Florencia served as Prior of the San Luis the Talimali mission and was a brilliant chronicle writer. Friar Francisco Marrón, on the other hand, had the distinction of serving as vicar of St. Augustine.

During the early colonial period, Florida's dependency on Cuba was almost complete. For almost two and a half centuries, Spanish Florida was intimately tied to Cuba. This dependency was due in part to Florida's lack of resources and in part to the Spanish crown's decision to maintain Florida as a garrison outpost for the protection of its other more valuable and wealthy Latin American colonies. This decision forced Florida to depend for its economic survival on the nearest Spanish colony — Cuba. St. Augustine depended on a little commerce and a monetary subsidy from Cuba sent by the Spanish crown to cover the colony's expenses. From the early sixteenth century until the creation of the Dioceses of St. Augustine in 1870, Florida's church affairs were under the direct jurisdiction of the bishop of Cuba; it wasn't until the eighteenth century that an auxiliary bishop of Santiago de Cuba resided in Florida.

During most of the Spanish colonial period, Florida was governed from Havana. From 1571 to 1763, thirty-five men served as governors of Florida. Three of them, Laureano de Torres y Ayala (1693–1699), Juan de Ayala y Escobar (1717–1718), and Manuel José de Justiz (1737), were born in Cuba. Later, one more Cuban-born governor, José Coppinger (1816–1821), was to serve as the last governor of Spanish Florida. In all those years, with the exception of the chain of missions and small settlements at Pensacola and San Marcos de Apalachee, St. Augustine was the only settlement of importance in Florida.

Beginning in the early part of the sixteenth century, the populations of Cuba and Florida migrated back and forth easily. This constant movement of people between Spanish Florida and Cuba, while never large in itself, was crucial in the creation of a durable commercial and human bond between these two communities. Most of Florida's trade and commerce took place with Cuba, thereby reinforcing the link that was established with the island. The strength of this link was tested by the British occupation period, but it was not broken.

In 1762, as part of the Seven Years' War (1756–1763), a British expeditionary force under the Earl of Albermarle, consisting of a fleet of over two hundred ships and twenty thousand soldiers and sailors, crossed the Atlantic and seized the Cuban capital. The British occupation of Havana, although brief in duration, had a dramatic impact on the future relations of Cuba and Florida.

First, the British invasion created a sense of nationalism as all of Cuba's ethnic groups fought together against a foreign invasion. Second, the British decision to open the city of Havana to international trade greatly stimulated the island's economy and commerce. The increase in economic activity lead the Cubans to realize that Spanish trade controls and restrictions were not in Cuba's best interest. This undermined further their loyalty to the Spanish crown. Finally, with the British military's occupation of Cuba also came the first political immigration from Cuba to Florida.

Among these early immigrants was the man who is considered to be the first Cuban political refugee to arrive in Florida: Pedro Morell de Santa Cruz — the bishop of Havana. Because of his unwillingness to submit to British rule, he was arrested and expelled from Cuba. He fled to St. Augustine in December of 1762 — the first in a long line of notable Cubans to seek refuge in Florida. He was admired not only for his service as bishop of Havana but also for being one of the best chroniclers of his time. His most important achievement was his work *Historia de la Isla y Catedral de Cuba*. Not only does it include a history of the Catholic Church on the island, but it also includes the first epic poem known to have been written in Cuba: "Espejo de paciencia." The poem was written by Silvestre de Balboa Troya y Quesada in 1608, but it had been forgotten in the archives of the Cathedral of Cuba in Santiago until Morell de Santa Cruz found it in 1760, two years before his exile to Florida.

The poem narrates the kidnapping of the bishop Cabezas y Altamirano by the French pirate named Gilberto Girón in 1604; it praises the bishop's rescue and the death of Girón at the hands of a Cuban black slave named Salvador Golomon. Bishop Cabezas, we should note, was the first bishop to visit Florida, when he toured Florida's Spanish mission in 1606. This poem is the first in defining the Cuban consciousness and the struggle for independence; its discovery by Pedro Morell marked the birth of an independent Cuban consciousness.

Our anthology begins with another exceptional individual who came to Florida almost a century later, Felix Varela y Morales. As a scholar, teacher, theologian, and writer, Varela played a crucial role in the development of philosophy and education in America. As a young boy, he participated in the reverse migration to Florida of the 1780s, when the territory was returned to Spanish hands after a twenty-year British occupation.

Varela was the son of a distinguished military family. Born in Cuba, he was brought to St. Augustine by his father when he was four years old. His grandfather, Bartolomé Morales, was in charge of the Spanish garrison there and later served as interim governor of Florida. Varela later returned to Cuba and studied at Havana's prestigious Colegio y Seminario de San Carlos y San Ambrosio. At the age of twenty-four, he took holy orders, becoming a priest and a professor of philosophy. In 1822, Varela was elected as a deputy to represent Cuba at the Spanish Cortes (parliament). His views against the Spanish monarchy landed him in trouble, and, in 1823, he was forced into exile.

As a scholar, philosopher, and theologian in New York, Varela continued his campaign for Cuba's independence from Spain. He became a symbol for Cuba's liberal intellectuals and trained a generation of Cuba's philosophers to search for independent solutions to Cuba's problems. In 1824, he began the publication of the magazine *El Habanero*, and later, with José Antonio Saco, he edited *El Mensajero Semanal,* which created a middle ground on which all Cuban patriots could meet and discuss issues relevant to Cuba. He also published two English-language magazines, *The Youth Friend* and *The Truth Teller,* in defense of the Catholic faith, which suffered frequent verbal and physical attacks during this period in the United States.

Varela was also influential in promoting the educational, political, and philosophical development of all of Latin America. In addition to writing and translating many textbooks of grammar and science, he translated into Spanish Thomas Jefferson's *Manual Of Parliamentary Procedures*. His most famous work, *Letters To Elpidio,* is a two-volume collection of letters which consist of philosophical and personal commentaries on the irreligiosity, superstition, and fanaticism of the times.

In poor health, after thirty years of serving poor parishioners in New York, Varela retired to the city where he had spent his childhood: St. Augustine. He lived there humbly, yet he was still greatly loved by his parishioners, who often visited him. In 1835, Varela died and was buried at the Tolomato cemetery in St. Augustine, where Cubans had a chapel built in his honor. To this date, many are still trying to canonize him.

By the time Varela died, it had become obvious that the new American republic was willing to confront Spain and other European nations for North American hegemony. The U.S. began extending its control to the adjacent territories. Its expansionist push to the west and south was made at the expense of Spanish territories, raising tension levels and complicating the already strained relations between the two nations. Eventually, the Spanish authorities surrendered to the inevitable and allowed the United States to obtain Florida in exchange for the cancellation of $5 million in claims and concessions.

On July 10, 1821, José Coppinger — Spanish Florida's last governor — had the unpleasant honor of officially turning over East Florida to U.S. Army Colonel Robert Butler, thus ending three centuries of Spanish occupation. Ironically, José Coppinger was born in Cuba, and, after releasing Florida to U.S. rule, he and most of Florida's Spanish residents returned to the island.

The Spanish presence in Florida during the next half century was reduced to only a small Minorcan colony that remained in St. Augustine, as well as a handful of Spanish and Cuban fishermen who stayed in the Tampa area and on some of the isolated keys. Meanwhile, interestingly enough, in Cuba, the town of Cárdenas, on the island's northern coast, was founded during this time mainly by Florida refugees.

As the nineteenth century progressed, a new city, Key West, emerged as a unique island community with a distinctive ethnic and cultural history. The first inhabitants to settle in large numbers, after Florida's territorial government was established by the United States in 1821, were seamen from New England and the Bahamas who lived by fishing and salvaging ships wrecked on the nearby reefs. The economic basis of the island was later diversified with the creation of a sponging industry and the first cigar-manufacturing plant.

The economic prosperity brought by the cigar industry was critical in developing the literary and cultural presence of Cubans in Florida. Among the first Cuban immigrants was a man who played a major role in the development of the cigar-manufacturing industry. A Spaniard by birth, Vicente Martínez Ybor arrived in Key West and founded V. M. Ybor and Company. There, he continued the production of his "El Principe de Gales"-brand cigar which he had produced in Cuba. Ybor then started receiving shipments of Cuban tobacco and organized a New York leaf-distribution office with other Cuban cigar manufacturers who had migrated there. Having opened the Havana-Key West-New York cigar production and distribution connection, he laid the foundation for the surge of prosperity that was to embrace Key West, and later Ybor City and Tampa.

The outbreak of the Ten Years' War for Cuban Independence from Spain further augmented the Cuban presence in Florida and the United States. During the Ten Years' War, from 1868 to 1878, the first large Cuban immigration to the United States in the nineteenth century took place. It was significant because approximately a tenth of the Cuban population was forced to flee in order to escape Spanish persecution and the effects of the war. These Cuban immigrants established strong enclaves in New York, Philadelphia, New Orleans, Charleston, Baltimore, and particularly Key West.

Due to its geographic proximity, Key West became the ideal location to receive the majority of the Cuban emigrant flow. By 1870, the Cuban population in Key West had grown to eleven hundred. Six years later, the key's population had swelled to over twelve thousand, with Cubans constituting a clear majority and Spanish becoming the city's second language.

The impact of the Cubans was far-reaching and had a powerful effect on Florida's entire economy. They helped transform Key West into a major nineteenth-century industrial community; cigar production brought an economic boom and an unprecedented era of prosperity that earned Key West the reputation as the "Havana cigar capital of the world."

Upon their arrival in Key West and later Ybor City, the skilled cigar workers enjoyed good working conditions and earned good salaries. A cigar worker could earn $15 to $20 per week, and some packers could make as much as $50 per week. The success of the cigar workers helped to fuel political, cultural, and literary interest among the Cubans. For example, the workers themselves hired readers, or *lectores,* a practice originating in Cuba.

The lectores were readers who spent the whole day seated in a loft above the cigar makers, reading aloud from newspapers, novels, and literary classics. Since most of the cigar workers of that time could neither read nor write, the lectores became the most important exponents of literature and culture in the average worker's life.

The readers were in a class all by themselves, not being part of the cigar factories' payroll; their salaries were paid, instead, by a weekly contribution of 25 cents from the cigar workers themselves. Most readers earned an average of $80 a week; a newspaper editor working as a reader could earn upwards of $125 a week. Using the cigar factory pulpits as a medium for the dissemination of political ideas, including the ideal of Cuban independence, the readers were often accused of inciting political strife and anti-Spanish sentiment.

The adoption of the reader system in the cigar-manufacturing plants had a revolutionary impact on Key West's, and later Tampa's, literary activity. First of all, the readers provided a market for the skills of Cuban journalists and writers who had just arrived in Florida. For many writers, such as Bonifacio Byrne in Ybor City and Martín Morúa Delgado in Key West, it was their main source of livelihood. Secondly, the reader system stimulated the proliferation of a wide variety of local Spanish-language newspapers and magazines.

In 1870, two editors who started their careers in Key West as readers, Juan María Reyes and José Dolores Poyo, founded Key West's first Spanish-language newspaper: *El Republicano.* Poyo later edited and published a Spanish-language propaganda newspaper from 1876 to 1898, named *El Yara,* which openly supported the Cuban independence movement. So open was the support of Florida's cigar makers to the Cuban independence movement that Spanish authorities constantly complained to U.S. officials.

At the peak of tensions, publisher/editor Juan María Reyes became the center of international attention. In 1870, he challenged Gonzalo Casteñón, the editor of the pro-Spanish, Havana-based newspaper *La Voz de Cuba,* and the leader of the Spanish "Voluntarios" (militias), to a duel. Casteñón accepted the challenge and sailed to Key West. But before he could meet his challenger, he was assassinated at the Russell House hotel by an unknown assailant. Casteñón's death became a "causa celebre" for the Spanish militia and a symbol of Spanish intransigence.

A year later, several freshmen students from the University of Havana Medical School were accused of desecrating Casteñón's crypt in the Espada cemetery in Havana. To appease the outrage of the Spanish militia, eight of the students were executed by firing squad and others were given harsh prison sentences. The brutality and senselessness of the incident became a symbol of the Spanish atrocities. When José Martí visited Tampa in 1892, in commemoration of the anniversary of the execution of the university students, he gave the speech "Los Pinos Nuevos" (The New Pines) that we have included in our anthology.

November 27th — the date of the executions — is still commemorated in Cuba.

Anti-Spanish sentiment remained strong in Cuba, and Cuban exiles in Florida played a significant role in fueling these sentiments. Writers often voiced their views on the future of Cuba at conferences or in newspaper articles. The San Carlos Institute played an important role by holding conferences and meetings on a regular basis. The cigar workers were deeply committed to the Cuban cause for freedom as well, and regularly contributed from their salaries to the cause. So much money was collected by Key West's cigar makers that the city was considered the main rebel center against Spain in the United States.

At the conclusion of the Ten Years' Wars, although the insurgents failed to gain independence for Cuba, the Spanish government was forced to make some concessions to the rebels. The peace treaty known as the "Pact of Zanjón" was signed in 1878; as a result, some of the Cuban exiles were able to return home. The time they had been living in the United States, however, served to strengthen the relationship between Cuba and the permanent Cuban enclaves that remained in Florida. The bond between Cuba and Florida was further enhanced during the postwar period.

During the first two decades of this postwar period, Cuban migration to the United States was again renewed. The political and economic situation in Cuba continued to deteriorate. Spanish colonial repression was on the increase, and thousands of Cubans left their homeland once again. They headed for the established Cuban enclave at Key West, and the newer Cuban communities in Jacksonville, Ocala, and Ybor City, as well as communities in Atlanta, Boston, and Chicago.

Among the Cubans who fled the island for Key West after the Ten Years' War was the noted journalist and novelist Martín Morúa Delgado. Morúa Delgado was the son of a slave and became one of the most influential black writers and intellectuals of his time. He had been implicated in the conspiracy of "La Guerra Chiquita of 1878," which followed the Ten Years' War, and was imprisoned in 1880. After his release, he emigrated to Key West. Life was difficult on the key, but he managed to get a position as a reader in a cigar factory, even though up to that point no Afro-Cuban had held that status. He also worked as a translator and regularly published pieces in magazines in Key West and New York. He wrote on a variety of issues, particularly about racism and the need for Cuban independence from Spain. Morúa Delgado returned to Cuba after independence and was elected to the Cuban Congress in 1901 and to the Senate in 1902. He later rose to become the president of the Cuban Senate in 1909 — the last black man in Cuba to hold that high office. His years in Florida were significant in shaping his literary and political reputation.

The exact number of Cubans who migrated to the United States during the peaceful years between the Cuban wars of independence is not known with certainty, since Cuban workers were not required to pass through customs or immigration processing centers. The physical proximity of Cuba to Florida and the low transportation cost from Havana to Key West and Tampa made the passage to Florida convenient and inexpensive. The high demand for skilled tobacco workers also made it possible for Cuban workers to emigrate to Florida with relative ease. Cuban workers would come to Florida when the workload required their assistance and return home during the slack periods and holidays.

In 1892, a U.S. congressional Cuba-Florida immigration investigating committee estimated that between fifty and a hundred thousand persons passed annually from Cuba to the United States and back again. Ramon William, American consul general to Cuba throughout the 1880s-1890s also testified:

> The people here (Cuba) look upon Florida as so much as a part of their own country. . . . They have more attachment for the U.S. than that sort of people (birds of passage). . . . I should say that there is no emigration from the island of Cuba in the European sense of the word, i.e., there is no emigrant class. There is a steerage, but they go as regular passengers. Between Key West and Havana, people go as between Albany and New York. . . . They go back and forth as those French laborers go from Canada into New England. . . . There is daily intercourse between the people of Key West and Tampa, Florida. (in Mormino 76)

Given the constant and traditional flow of Cubans between Florida and the island, a stable population of Cubans simply settled and formed their own communities in Florida.

Although the cigar boom made Key West's future appear bright, growing labor tensions and unrest resulted in the most devastating strike in the city's history — the six-month labor strike of 1885. When the news spread of Key West's continuous labor problems, various attractive offers were sent to Key West's cigar factory owners to visit Pensacola, Mobile, Galveston, and Tampa for possible relocation sites. Vicente Martínez Ybor was observing the events and took action near Tampa.

At first, Martínez Ybor constructed only a two-story building to accommodate a cigar factory and some small houses to serve as homes for workers. When the great fire in 1886 destroyed his main factory in Key West, Ybor decided to leave Key West altogether and move his entire operation to Tampa. The area became known as Ybor City. Upon Ybor's departure, most of his Key West workers followed him, creating a population shift to the new cigar factories in Ybor City.

The labor strikes and the fire of 1886 had a detrimental effect on Key West's economy in other ways. Although the city quickly rebuilt, the island's monopoly on cigar production had been broken; besides Ybor City, other competitive cigar centers were formed in West Tampa, Jacksonville, and Ocala. The predominance of Key West as the cigar capital of the world had begun to decline, and the exodus of cigar makers to other production centers devastated Key West's cigar industry and its economy. Key West's population declined from twenty-one thousand to fifteen thousand in the two-year period preceeding 1895. Tampa would eventually become the major producer of cigars in Florida.

Tampa had been a small, isolated, peaceful village whose only source of commerce was the export of fish to Havana and the shipment of pine to Plant City for shipment to other markets. Tampa's population did not exceed 720 people in 1885, but four years after the founding of Ybor City, the population had increased to 5,532 — a figure which included 1,313 Cubans.

Gradually, the Cubans adjusted to their new surroundings, and, within a short time after its establishment, Ybor City resembled a small part of Havana transplanted to Tampa. Social and fraternal clubs were soon organized. In April 1890, El Liceo Cubano was formally opened as a literary, artistic, and recreation center. As the Cubans consolidated their hold and influence on one of the area's economic underpinnings, cigar manufacturing, they continued to immerse themselves in the crusade for Cuban independence.

A constant visitor to Tampa at this time was the Cuban revolutionary and writer José Martí. Without a doubt, Martí is one of the most important figures in Cuban history and literature. The son of Spanish parents, Martí began writing at an early age. At sixteen, he was imprisoned for political reasons, and, after serving several months of hard labor, he was sent into exile in Spain.

In 1881, after traveling through Europe and Latin America, Martí finally settled in New York, where he concentrated on his writing and on organizing the struggle for Cuba's independence. As a writer, Martí is known for his journalistic articles and is also highly acclaimed as the precursor of the Modernist movement in literature.

During the three-year period from 1892 to 1895, Martí visited Ybor City at least seventeen times. He spearheaded the formation of revolutionary clubs there and other cities in Florida. He spoke of the need for unity in the creation of a free and greater Cuba. He wanted not only a free nation, but a new nation with democratic and egalitarian values. The cigar workers in Florida responded passionately to his call.

In Key West, Martí founded the Partido Revolucionario Cubano (PRC) and directed all his energies toward organizing the war effort against Spain. Besides Key West and Ybor City, Martí also visited Jacksonville, Ocala, and St. Augustine, organizing revolutionary clubs and raising money for the armed insurrection. He was always welcomed with large crowds, speaking before groups of thousands. Martí also founded and directed the newspaper *Patria*, published in New York, which was solely devoted to the cause of Cuban independence and was widely read in the tobacco factories of Florida.

The Cuban cigar workers constituted the main body of support for the Cuban independence movement. A handful of dedicated Cuban intellectuals, journalists, and writers in the United States provided its leadership. Eloquent and dynamic leaders edited newspapers, organized political cells and revolutionary clubs, raised money to finance the war effort, and, as lectores, kept the faith alive by reading inspiring stories of the Ten Years' War, the French Revolution, and the biographies of distinguished Latin American war heroes from their factory pulpits.

Spanish-language newspapers played an immense role for Cuban readers by disseminating information about conditions in the homeland as well as information concerning local affairs, much as they still do today. Furthermore, they were the only vehicle for writers to publish their poetry and essays while living abroad.

In the migration of cigar workers from Key West to Ybor City came José Dolores Poyo, who brought with him his newspaper, *El Yara*, begun in 1869 in Key West. Although its existence in Tampa was brief, it was the first Spanish-language publication started in Tampa. *El Yara* was followed by the weekly newspaper *La Revista de la Florida*, which was published by Ramón Rivero Rivero starting in 1888.

Rivero was a Cuban journalist and lector at a cigar factory who lived in Key West before moving to Tampa. In Tampa, he published another Ybor City newspaper called *Cuba*, from 1887 to 1898, which served as a voice for José Martí's Cuban Revolutionary Party. Meanwhile, Néstor Leonelo Carbonell edited another newspaper entitled *La Contienda*, which made its appearance in 1890.

A large number of small Spanish-language newspapers were published in Key West and Ybor City during this time. They represented a wide variety of ideologies ranging from anarchism to socialism, but generally they all focused on the struggle for Cuban independence. Besides serving as a tool for promoting political ideologies, these newspapers also served as a vehicle for writers to express their voice, otherwise impossible for them while residing in an English-speaking environment. Among the more important of these newspapers were *La Revista de Cayo Hueso, El Intransigente, La Tribuna del Pueblo, La Unión Cubana, Verdad, El Esclavo, La Revista de Cuba Libre, El Mosquito, El Independiente, El Patriota,* and *El Crítico de Ybor City.*

Néstor Leonelo Carbonell had arrived in Key West in 1889 and worked as a teacher and journalist. He later moved to Tampa where he established a school. He also owned a small bookstore called The Literary Gallery, which supplied readers with books and newspapers. His store became a literary meeting place. Carbonell was instrumental in creating the Cuban Lyceum (Liceo Cubano), which became a literary and artistic society with a night school, at which he taught. The endeavors of these editors and teachers were essential to the literary development of Cubans in Florida.

The difficulty of obtaining up-to-date news and information in Spanish was overcome for Hispanic residents when reader/journalist Ramón Valdespino, with the assistance of Victor E. Muñoz Rivera, began translating into Spanish the articles and telegraphic dispatches which had appeared in the English-language press the previous day. The name of this gazette was *La Traducción* and its publication lasted until the mid-1950s. *El Diario de Las Americas* and *El Nuevo Herald* continue this tradition today in Dade County in south Florida.

Cuban passion for politics in Key West and Tampa was not limited to the pro-independence movement on the island. Cuban political clout and power often spilled over to local and state politics. Political participation of Cuban immigrants was made possible by the fact that, although U.S. laws required five years' residency before foreigners could become citizens, state elections required only a one-year residency, and local elections only six months. This short residency requirement, coupled with the political influence of the cigar factory lectores and other community leaders, allowed the Cubans to exercise considerable political leverage in both Monroe and Hillsborough Counties, where Key West and Tampa are located.

In 1875, for example, the 1,032 registered Cuban voters in Monroe County, Florida, were largely responsible for electing Key West's first Cuban mayor, Carlos

Manuel de Céspedes, Jr., son of the hero of the Ten Years' War. Furthermore, Manuel Patricio Delgado, Manuel Moreno, Gonzalo Pompes, and Fernando Figueredo were all elected to the Florida legislature, the first Cubans in the nineteenth century to hold such legislative posts in the state.

The Cuban residents of Ybor City also actively participated in local politics. On more than one occasion, Cubans were elected to public offices in Hillsborough County's municipal government. Ramón Rivero y Rivero, the well-known editor of the newspapers *El Yara* and *Revista de La Florida,* was a delegate from Hillsborough County to the National Convention of the Republican Party in 1890. Many other Cubans and Cuban-Americans were also elected or appointed to top-ranking political positions throughout the state of Florida.

In 1870, Alejandro Mendoza was the first Cuban to be appointed to a Monroe County government position — that of justice of the peace. The following year, Juan María Reyes, the editor of *El Republicano,* was also appointed to that position. Three more Cubans would also be named justices of the peace in Key West; at least one of them, Angel de Lono, became a county judge. Other Cubans appointed to high political positions were Manuel Govin, who was appointed postmaster of Jacksonville in 1876, and Issac Carrillo, who was named southern district attorney. In 1887, Cándido Angel Martínez, son of the founder of Ybor City, was elected alderman in Tampa's municipal election.

On May 18, 1895, the day on which José Martí died in an insignificant skirmish in Cuba, the legislature of the state of Florida recognized the suburb of West Tampa, another city near Ybor City, as a separate municipality. The town, founded by Cubans, had grown in such an extraordinary manner that it had converted itself into a prosperous town with sufficient means to exist independently. Almost all the inhabitants of West Tampa were of Cuban origin, and they were politically active, electing Fernando Figueredo their first mayor. Figueredo had earlier served as a state representative for Monroe County. Although he was a veteran of Cuba's Ten Years' War, a disillusioned Figueredo sought exile in Florida in 1878. He became a naturalized citizen and later served as Hillsborough's superintendent of schools from 1895 to 1899.

When independence was achieved, Figueredo returned to Cuba and continued a successful political career. He became secretary of the interior and later secretary of the treasury. He is best remembered for his narrations of the historical account of the military and political aspects of the Ten Years' War in his *La Toma de Bayamo* and *La Revolución del Yara* (1902) as well as the biography *Pedro Figueredo.*

With the outbreak of the Spanish-American war, new exiles continued to arrive in Florida. These included the Borrero family, who arrived at Key West in 1896, shortly after the beginning of the War of Independence. It was forced to emigrate to Key West because of Dr. Borrero's anti-Spanish revolutionary activities. Esteban Borrero Echevarría was a Cuban poet, essay writer, and educator. Upon his arrival, Esteban Borrero became involved in exile revolutionary activities while continuing his literary career. He taught at the Club San Carlos and published many essays and poems during his exile in Key West. Esteban Borrero was also the father of two accomplished young poets: Juana Borrero and Dulce María Borrero. Dulce María returned to Cuba after the war and continued to write and work as an activist for education and women's rights.

The Borreros' oldest daughter, Juana, whose work we have included in the anthology, went on to become the most celebrated member of this literary family. She is considered to be one of the best female poets of her time. At the early age of twelve, she began writing poetry. Her best-known works are the poems "Las Hijas del Ran," "Apollo," and "La Ultima Rima," the latter written and published in Key West. She died of typhoid fever and was buried on the key in 1896 at the age of eighteen, but not before she had gained a reputation as an important poet in Cuba's literary legacy.

Another notable Cuban poet to come to Key West during this period was Diego Vicente Tejera. Tejera was a lecturer, an essayist, and a poet. During his stay in Key West, he published regularly in Key West and New York newspapers, and translated the works of major writers such as Heine, Goethe, Leopardi, and Longfellow into Spanish. Tejera was instrumental in maintaining the pro-independence fervor alive in the exile community after Martí's death.

The traditional Cuba-Florida ties were once again reinforced with the entry of the United States into the Spanish-American war and the United States' nascent expansionist tendencies. Florida became a major staging area for the Cuban campaign. During the spring and summer of 1898, the ports at Fernandina, Jacksonville, Tampa, and Key West served as the staging areas for thousands of U.S. soldiers destined to participate in the invasion of Cuba.

Tampa also became headquarters of the Cuban revolutionaries when Tomás Estrada Palma, José Martí's successor to the junta in New York, ordered all able young and healthy unmarried Cuban men disposed to aid the rebel cause to make their way to Tampa. Forty Cubans from Jacksonville, two hundred from New York, and 150 from Key West convoyed from Tampa to join the insurrection in Cuba.

Many notable Cuban writers also joined the Cuban Liberation Army, either prior to the U.S. entering into the conflict or upon Estrada Palma's call to arms after the American declaration of war. While many of them distinguished themselves in the battlefield and rose to high ranks in the Cuban Liberation Army, some of them met their death on the battlefield. José Martí, Cuba's most important writer and the main organizing force behind the Cuban independence movement, is the best-known casualty of the war.

Cuban residents of Ocala tried to immortalize Martí by organizing a new municipality named Martí City in September, 1894. The assembly elected new public officials; all, with the exception of the secretary, were Cuban natives. In June 1896, however, Martí City was dealt a fatal blow as the city's cigarmakers, unable to compete with Ybor City's production and prices, were compelled to abandon their factories and move to Tampa.

Another Cuban writer who lived in Florida and fought in the War of Independence of 1895 was José Manuel Carbonell. Raised and educated in Tampa, Carbonell is noted for founding the newspaper *El Expedicionario* in Key West and for editing, later in Cuba, his monumental work *La Evolución De La Cultura Cubana (1628-1927)*. This last work was a comprehensive treatment of all aspects of Cuban cultural development, including lyrical and patriotic poetry, oratory, and essays. Carbonell returned to Florida after the 1959 revolution and died in Miami in 1968, during his second migration to the United States.

Though not included in this literary anthology, Gerardo Castellanos y García deserves mention. He was born in Key West in 1879 and lived there until 1899, when, at twenty years of age, he migrated to Cuba. In Cuba, he wrote numerous historical essays and books, including *Motivos de Cayo Hueso,* on the history of the Cuban migration to Key West, his city of birth.

The next turbulent period, following the Cuban/Spanish- American war, motivated many writers, such as Bonifacio Byrne, to speak out. The end result of the War of 1898 was the successful secession of Cuba from Spain, but at a tremendous cost in both human life and the total devastation of the nation's economy. War-related deaths were estimated at more than three hundred thousand, well over a tenth of the island's population. The Cuban economy was ruined as a result of the scourge campaign waged by the Cuban insurgents.

Almost thirty years of wars, uprisings, and rebellions left Cuba spiritually, physically, and economically drained. Its principal political and military leaders had been killed; the physical destruction was devastating; and at the end of the war, the country was under U.S. military occupation.

When independence was finally granted to the Cubans, on May 20, 1902, the United States left the door open for future intervention through the imposition of a constitutional appendix known as the Platt Amendment; this amendment literally turned Cuba into an American protectorate. Thus, when Tomás Estrada Palma was elected as Cuba's first president, the Cuban people discovered they had achieved self-government without achieving self-determination. They had gained independence without becoming sovereign.

Bonifacio Byrne was among the first poets to capture the new nation's feelings of frustration and disappointment. Byrne, like many of his compatriots, fled Cuba at the beginning of the War of Independence. While living in Tampa, he worked as a lector in a tobacco factory and dedicated himself to the separatist cause. Byrne founded the "Club Revolucionario de Tampa," in addition to contributing political articles.

After the war, he sailed from Tampa for Havana in 1899; as he approached the island, he was shocked to see a ship flying both the Cuban and the United States flag. This image upon his return, compounded with the optimism he had felt while living in Tampa and hearing of the success of the war, prompted him to write his most famous poem, "Mi Bandera," in which he denounces the U.S. military occupation of Cuba.

In spite of troubled times at home, the end of the war signaled the return of thousands of exiles to Cuba to contribute to the reconstruction of their devastated nation. For many Cubans, however, the decision to return to a war-devastated Cuba was met with little enthusiasm. Many Cubans had been living in exile for up to thirty years; Jacksonville, Key West, Miami, Tampa, Ocala, and West Palm Beach had become their new home. Returning to Cuba meant giving up the security of their jobs and established businesses to start over in an economically devastated country which had become foreign, to them and their American-born children. Thus, many Cubans remained in the United States, transforming their exile enclaves into permanent Cuban-American communities.

By the end of the century, these nineteenth-century Cuban immigrants had made many outstanding contributions to their communities and to the state of Florida. Cuban immigrants were credited with founding Florida's cigar industry and making it one of the state's main source of income. They also founded the first bilingual and integrated school in the country: the school at the Club San Carlos Institute in Key West, funded by both the U.S. and Cuban governments until 1959, and remaining open until 1971 with private donations. They founded the state's first labor union, and participated actively in state, county, and local politics. In summary, they made significant contributions to the social and cultural life of their Florida communities. Writers participated in this process through their efforts as factory readers, essayists, orators, editors, translators, and teachers.

The Cuban exile enclaves of the nineteenth century that began as temporary sanctuaries to escape political persecution became permanent, vibrant, and influential communities. These Cuban-American communities would leave a strong cultural, economic, and political legacy for future generations.

During the first decades of the new Cuban republic, the American military intervention, with its political, economic, and cultural penetration, set the groundwork for a renewed U.S.–Cuban relationship which strengthened once more the traditional Florida-Cuba links.

Those commercial and cultural ties were further cemented in 1913, when two pioneers, Domingo Rosillo and Agustín Parla, the latter a Cuban from Key West, were the first to cross the Florida straits by air. The Rosillo-Parla crossing opened the airways, thus making the Florida-Havana passage a fast and convenient means of transportation. In the 1920s, the two communities became even closer when regular flights between Key West and Cuba were initiated. By the end of the decade, a network of maritime ports and airports wove the island of Cuba and the Florida peninsula into a casual and neighborly relationship. American tourists would go vacationing to Havana, while their Cuban counterparts sought the advantages of Florida's shopping, business opportunities, and, from time to time, safety as a political haven.

The early years of the young Cuban republic also witnessed a nation assailed by political instability, frequent revolts, and continued U.S. meddling in its internal affairs. The end result of such a combination of factors would be a renewed political migration to the United States. Just as in the previous migrations, most Cuban refugees would once again seek refuge in the place that traditionally had been their sanctuary, Florida.

The first Cuban political migration in the twentieth century began in 1917, when General José Miguel Gómez — Cuba's second president — started a rebellion against the reelection of his successor, Mario García Menocal, precipitating the second American military intervention and forcing Gómez to seek refuge in Miami. Soon after that incident, for a variety of reasons, many Cuban dissidents once again began to leave Cuba in large numbers.

The first post-independence generation of exile writers was very different. With the relative success of the pro-independence movement, the literary effort lost its principal source of inspiration. From the mid-1920s on, the political and economic consequences of the first world war and the growing discontent of the social condition of the nation became the main theme expressed by many poets and writers during this period.

Among such poets was Agustín Acosta. Although Acosta would not come to live in Florida until the latter part of his life, early in his career he began to write poems depicting the harsh life of the Cuban sugar workers. His work presaged the emergence of the socially conscious literature of the 1930s. Another poet and political activist who did reside in Florida during the 1920s and followed this literary trend was Rubén Martínez Villena.

In 1923, a young Rubén Martínez Villena, in the company of members of the prestigious National Veterans and Patriots Association, came to Florida to plot the overthrow of the government of President Alfredo Zayas y Alfonso. The conspirators planned to purchase an airplane from which to conduct bombing missions against the presidential palace in Havana and incite a rebellion to oust the Zayas government. Ironically, Zayas, also a poet, had been an exile himself in Key West during the struggle for Cuban independence.

The conspirators' plans failed, and Rubén Martínez Villena was arrested by U.S. authorities and sent to prison. After his release, he went to work in a beer factory in Ybor City. He later returned to Cuba and actively opposed the Machado regime. Because of his political activities and his Communist affiliations, he was arrested and served several prison terms there.

The 1920s and 1930s also saw a series of events that would have serious repercussions on the Cuban communities in Florida. First of all, technological advances made it possible to produce machine-made cigars at a cheaper price than the hand-rolled cigars, thus undermining the latter's market share. In addition, the rising popularity of cigarettes also contributed to the rapid decline of the hand-rolled cigar industry and its once-powerful Cuban manufacturing centers.

Secondly, the Florida factory owners got rid of the factory readers, whom they accused of spreading radical socialist and anarchist ideas. After a brief strike by factory workers — perhaps one of few strikes in American history over a cultural issue — the readers were replaced by radios. English-broadcast programs to the factories assisted the rapid assimilation of the Cuban community into mainstream American culture.

Finally, the great depression of 1929 had a devastating impact on the once-striving Cuban communities in Key West and Tampa. The U.S. government modified the labor immigration laws and introduced new reforms so restrictive that they practically denied admission to foreign workers. Cuban labor immigration almost ceased, and the Cuban enclaves in the U. S. would be denied the continuous flow of immigrants that was so important for their growth and vitality.

The combination of all those factors lead to a rapid decline in Key West's population, dropping from 18,749 in 1920 to 12,836 in 1930. The Tampa-based Cuban community faced a similar fate. Although benefiting from Key West's exodus, Tampa's Cuban community was being rapidly absorbed into the American mainstream by the dramatic growth of Tampa's non-Cuban population. While Tampa's Cuban population grew from 3,859 in 1910 to 5,112 in 1930, the city's population swelled dramatically from 37,782 to 101,161 in the same period.

During this difficult period, many Cubans — including readers, writers, journalists, and editors — returned to Cuba. Others remained in Florida. They adapted to the changing conditions and continued to publish their newspapers. An example of such a figure is Victoriano Mantegia, who emigrated to Florida in 1913 and worked as a reader in Tampa's cigar factories. He later became an editor, and in 1922, founded the newspaper *La Gaceta,* the longest-running Spanish-language newspaper in Florida, still in print today.

A writer born and raised in Tampa during this time was José Yglesias. Members of his family had come to Florida during the nineteenth century and remained as permanent residents of Ybor City and West Tampa. As an adult, Yglesias moved to New York and went on to become a prominent journalist and novelist, often writing in English about Cuba and his Cuban upbringing in Ybor City. For example, his novel *The Truth About Them,* published in 1971, deals with a Cuban family's arrival in Key West in the nineteenth century and its development there, and later in Ybor City, amid the cigar industry.

In the 1930s, as Key West and Ybor City declined, Miami, with a population of 110,637 and a boom in real estate, was growing very rapidly and becoming a principal city in south Florida. It soon emerged as the new center of Cuban influence. University students and other political activists who actively opposed the dictatorship of Gerardo Machado began arriving in waves seeking refuge from the political turmoil in the island.

After Machado's overthrow, most of the Cuban exiles who lived in Miami returned to Cuba; however, these were quickly replaced by a new group of exiles who had been Machado loyalists (including the former president himself, who died in Miami in 1939). In time, two other Cuban presidents and their supporters would come to settle in Florida: Fulgencio Batista (1899–1973), who lived in Daytona Beach after his presidential mandate ended in 1944, and Carlos Prio

Socarrás (1903–1979), whose government was overthrown by Batista himself in a bloodless coup in 1952. He later died in Miami.

With the return of Batista to power that year, the cycle repeated itself. Hundreds of sympathizers of the former democratic government and political opponents to the new Batista regime went into exile. Again, Florida became the central point of attraction for the majority of the new refugees. This time, however, Miami had replaced Key West and Tampa as the capital of Cuban exiles.

According to the U.S. Census, it was estimated that in 1950, there were 29,295 Cuban-born whites living in the United States, of which 7,910 resided in the state of Florida. The Cuban community in Florida, though suffering from the continuous process of cultural assimilation, was still able to revitalize itself by the periodic arrival of exiles and Cubans who came looking for business opportunities. By 1955, it was estimated that Cuban nationals had invested $150 million in south Florida, mostly in real estate.

In 1958, when Batista fled the country after a violent three-year struggle against opposition groups, the number of Cubans living in the United States had increased dramatically to approximately forty thousand. Among the many writers who had found refuge in Florida in the 1950s during the Batista years were poets Heberto Padilla, Martha Padilla, and Pura Del Prado.

Heberto Padilla was an aspiring poet during his first residency in Miami, where he lived and studied at the University of Miami. He returned to Cuba upon the fall of the Batista dictatorship and worked as a foreign correspondent for *Prensa Latina*. In Cuba, he co-founded *Revista Unión* and wrote articles for *Diario Revolución*. In 1970, Padilla received international attention when he was arrested and imprisoned in a controversy centered around his award-winning book *Fuera del Juego*. In 1980, Padilla and his wife, Belkis Cuza Malé, were finally allowed to leave Cuba, marking the beginning of his second period of exile.

His sister Martha Padilla migrated to Florida with her brother Heberto in 1956. She never returned to Cuba and presently lives in Georgia. She has published several volumes of poetry, including *Comitiva Al Crepúsculo, La Alborada Del Tigre,* and *Nuestro Gustavo Adolfo Becquer* in collaboration with three other Cuban women poets: Josefina Inclán, Pura del Prado, and Ana Rosa Núñez.

Pura del Prado migrated to the United States during this period as well. She left Cuba in 1958, after becoming involved in revolutionary activities against the Batista dictatorship. She, too, has published several volumes of poetry and has been featured in various anthologies. Her best-known works are *De Codo al Alcoiris, Canto a Martí,* and *Color de Orisha.*

In the 1950s, several Spanish-language publications still existed among the Cuban communities in Florida. In 1954, there were five Spanish-language publications serving the Cuban community in Ybor City. Among these were the previously mentioned *La Gaceta,* published since the mid-1920s by Victoriano Manteiga, and *Traducción-Prensa,* as well as three other publications: the semi-monthly magazine *Trópico* and two news weeklies: *Heraldo Dominical* and *El Internacional.*

Meanwhile, in Miami, publication of *Diario Las Américas* had begun in 1953. Although founded by a Nicaraguan journalist named Horacio Aguirre, the *Diario* would serve as a medium for many Cuban journalists such as Guillermo Martínez Márquez, Carlos Márquez Sterling, and Humberto Medrano, who made regular contributions to the paper throughout the years. The *Diario Las Américas* and, much later, *El Nuevo Herald,* as well as countless other small Spanish-language newspapers, continued the tradition of serving not only as a vital news medium, but also as a literary instrument for writers to reach the Spanish-speaking Cuban communities of south Florida.

Fidel Castro's revolutionary triumph in 1959 triggered the largest migration ever of Cubans to the United States. Between 1959 and 1990, close to a million Cubans emigrated to the United States. In keeping with the pattern of the nineteenth century, most of these exiles came for political reasons and chose Florida as a place of residency. Among them were many poets and prose writers. Little Havana, a small urban neighborhood near the Miami River and the downtown area of the city, became a port of entry for many Cuban refugees in the 1960s and 1970s. By the 1980s, most younger Cubans had moved out of Little Havana and populated major areas of West Miami, Kendall, and Hialeah. Others settled in Tampa, Ocala, and other Florida cities where Cuban communities already existed, though much more assimilated than in Miami.

Most of the new Cubans arriving in Florida after 1959 have remained in Miami. Cuban migration to Miami has continued to increase, not only because of Cubans from the island, but also because of Cubans living in other parts of the United States, such as New Jersey and Illinois, who are moving to Miami. In the last decades of the twentieth century, greater Miami has become a major urban center for Florida as well as an economic, political, and cultural focus for Cubans in exile everywhere. Over six hundred thousand Cubans presently live in greater Miami. Cubans and Cuban-Americans continue to work for the future of a democratic Cuba, but they are also critically involved in the development of south Florida. Since 1960, south Florida has seen Cubans as mayors, county managers, state and federal representatives, presidents of universities, presidents of banks and national companies, teachers, journalists, engineers, baseball players, dancers, actors, small business owners, factory workers, and, of course, poets and novelists. Every aspect of life in Greater Miami has been marked by the influence of Cubans.

In the last forty years, the Cuban presence in greater Miami has become so strong that literary avenues have blossomed like never before. Examples can be seen in the proliferation of Spanish bookstores such as Ediciones Universal and La Moderna Poesia, and in the growing Spanish-language sections at almost all English bookstores. Universities have developed centers for Cuban Studies and special library collections. Much of the latter effort is due to the work of Cuban librarians such as (to name only a few) Rosita Abella, Ana Rosa Núñez, and Lesbia Varona at the University of Miami and Rosa Mesa at the University of Florida. There are also literary gatherings, presses, magazines, and the internationally recognized Miami Book Fair International, which features a Spanish-language series. Cuban communities also continue to expand in Tampa, Ocala, Jacksonville, Orlando, and other Florida cities.

It is impossible to discuss such a large migration spanning three decades as if it consisted of a homogeneous group. Indeed, Cuban exiles reveal a myriad of cultural, political, social, and ideological layers. It is equally so for the writers. For the sake of clarification, we will speak of three groups of writers.

The first is composed of those writers born in the early decades of the twentieth century who achieved literary recognition in the 1920s, 1930s, and 1940s, thus reaching their peak literary production in Cuba before they went into exile in Miami. This group includes some of Cuba's most renowned literary figures. The oldest of these writers is Agustín Acosta, discussed previously. He was a member of the same generation as José Manuel Carbonell, Juana Borrero, and Rubén Martínez Villena; the latter had likewise spent part of their lives in Florida, but at younger ages.

Other writers included in this group represent the most notable literary figures in Cuban post-Colonial history: the poet Eugenio Florit, the short-fiction writers Enrique Labrador Ruiz and Carlos Montenegro, and the Afro-Cuban folklorist Lydia Cabrera. Even though these writers had produced their most important work while still living in Cuba, their presence in exile was influential to the cultural and literary development of younger Miami writers. They continued to publish in Miami, and many new editions of their major works were reprinted in exile, especially by Ediciones Universal, which has played an important role in promoting Cuban exile literature. Also, these writers often made guest appearances at literary forums, until they became too frail to do so; then they were visited by younger writers in their homes. Their presence in exile served as an inspiration to other generations abroad.

Eugenio Florit is most noted for being one of the leaders of the avant-garde "pure poets." Florit published his first book of poetry, *32 Poemas Breves,* in 1927. In the 1930s, Florit's adherence to pure poetry became stronger as is reflected in the poems gathered in the book *Trópico,* and more prevalent in *Doble Acento.* Florit published several works throughout Latin America, and his poems have appeared in numerous anthologies. He moved to New York in the 1940s and worked as both diplomat and later professor, until he retired in 1969. In 1982, he moved to Miami, where he lived until his death. He published two more collections of poetry while in Miami.

Enrique Labrador Ruiz is one of the most important figures in twentieth-century Cuban literature, and a precursor of the present-day Latin American novel. He was an innovator of the Cuban novel, overcoming traditional narrative schemes. In 1933, he published *El Laberinto de Si Mismo,* which marked the beginning of the Spanish-American experimental novel. He is also credited with being the precursor of magic realism with his short story "El Conejito Ulán," published in 1946. He recently died in Miami, where he lived in exile with his wife Che-Ché.

By contrast, Montenegro is representative of the social current in Cuban literature. His best-known novel, *Hombre Sin Mujeres,* narrates the violence and brutality of prison life and its tendency toward homosexuality. This narrative is considered by critics to be of extraordinary contemporary meaning. Montenegro went into exile in 1959 and moved to Miami in 1962, where he continued to publish and write until his death in 1981. He was best known for his short stories.

Lydia Cabrera is another extraordinary writer belonging to this group. She was an ethnologist, a researcher, and an Afro-Cuban folklore writer. She worked under the renowned Cuban anthropologist Fernando Ortiz and became the foremost authority on the stories and legends of the African Yoruba and Locumi slaves brought to Cuba and the Antilles. She went on to be the first writer to publish what is considered documentary Afro-Cuban narratives in her *Cuentos Negros de Cuba* (1940) and *Por Qué . . .* (1948). Cabrera's stories are, in reality, transcriptions of the oral narratives of the Afro-Cuban world, revealing the magic concept of the world brought to the Americas by African slaves. She continued to write and published extensively during her exile in Miami. She died in 1992.

Her works have been translated into many European languages, while only a few have been translated into English. There is now a renewed interest in her studies, due in part to the massive number of Cubans seeking refuge in Florida in the last three decades.

Because of sheer volume alone, it is logical to expect that the number of writers among these immigrants would increase as well. Indeed, since there are so many significant writers composing the last two groups included, we have had to make difficult choices in our selections for the anthology; we regret having omitted many writers due to spatial constraints or because of the historical parameters of the anthology, which spans slightly more than a century. We have, however, tried to at least mention in this introduction all the writers we were familiar with and apologize in advance for any omission.

The second and very broad group currently exiled is composed of writers who were born between the decades of the 1920s and 1940s, who were in the process of developing their literary reputations in 1959. Their ages place them within a generation that came to adulthood during the second Batista period, some much younger than others. Many joined the political opposition against Batista and later suffered the betrayals of the Castro revolution. They left the island at different times during the last three decades. Some have resided permanently in Miami since their arrival; others have lived in Miami on and off for extended periods of time. Their literary styles are heterogeneous, ranging from avant-garde abstract to social realism.

Exile writers who comprise this group include Ana Rosa Núñez, Felix Cruz-Alvarez, Angel Cuadra, Jorge Vals, Heberto Padilla (who went into exile a second time in 1980), Armando Alvarez Bravo, Mercedes García Tuduri, Hilda Perera, Juana Rosa Pita, Uva Clavijo, Gladys Zaldivar, Rita Geada, Teresa María Rojas, Belkis Cuza Malé, Amelia del Castillo, Ernesto Díaz Rodríguez, Mercedes Cortazar, Concha Alzola, Lillian Bertot, Esperanza Rubido, Carlos Alberto Montaner, and Reynaldo Arenas, who arrived in Florida in the 1980 Mariel exodus and made extended visits to Miami and Miami Beach throughout his ten years in exile.

Many of the writers in this group have also been involved with newspapers and literary publications. Writers such as Heberto Padilla, Carlos Alberto Montaner, Agustín Tamargo, Armando Alvarez Bravo, Uva Clavijo, Belkis Cuza Malé, to name only a few, write regular columns for *El Miami Herald* and *El Diario Las Américas*. Cuza Malé also directs the literary magazine *Linden Lane,* the longest running literary magazine in exile. Other literary magazines published in the U.S. since 1959 include *Mariel,* started by Reynaldo Arenas and other Mariel writers and artists such as Juan Abreu and Carlos Victoria (who reside in Miami) as well as Reinaldo García Ramos and Roberto Valero; *La Nuez,* directed by Rafael Bordao; *Lyra,* directed by Lourdes Gil and Iraida Iturralde; and *Latino Stuff Review,* founded by Nilda Cepero in Miami.

Finally, we have the last group of writers born in Cuba or the United States from the 1950s until the 1970s. These writers would have been raised primarily in exile, or in Cuba during the revolution. Many of those raised in Cuba arrived in Miami during the Mariel boatlift or in the early years of the 1990s, when Cuba's economic decline progressed dramatically. The latter are still in the process of gaining recognition in the Florida community. Others spent some of their childhood in different U.S. cities or in Madrid, as in the case of Amando Fernández. Because of the variety of experiences, this is probably the most linguistically heterogeneous group. It includes writers such as Silvia Curbelo, a resident of Tampa who writes only in English, as well as poets such as Amando Fernández, who wrote exclusively in Spanish, since he spent most of his life in Spain before arriving in Miami as a young adult. Gustavo Peréz-Firmat, on the other hand, was raised in Coral Gables, Florida, resides in North Carolina today, and alternates between languages.

We can include in this group writers who have lived or are living in diverse cities throughout the state of Florida, for example: in Miami, Ricardo Pau-Llosa, Carolina Hospital, Amando Fernández, Carlos Victoria, Lourdes Tomás, Sandra Castillo, Ivonne Lamazares, Marisella Veiga, Richard Blanco, Liz Balmaseda, Anthony Pérez, Adrián Castro, Orlando González-Esteva, Raquel Puig-Zaldivar, Daina Chaviano, Pablo Medina, and Gustavo Peréz- Firmat (raised in Miami who insists he is a Miami poet though he teaches in North Carolina); in Tampa, Silvia Curbelo and Dionisio Martínez; in Tallahassee, Roberto Fernández (raised in Palm Beach) and Virgil Suárez, both professors at Florida State University; and in Orlando, lawyer Javier Fraxeda who published his first novel *The Lonely Crossing of Juan Cabrera* in 1993.

The nature of literary life in the United States makes it extremely difficult to make a living as a writer, unless one produces a fiction bestseller such as *The Mambo Kings Play Songs of Love,* written by a Cuban-American from New York, Oscar Hijuelos (the book won a Pulitzer Prize and was made into a film). Consequently, the majority of the writers from this group — and the preceding one for that matter — teach at colleges and universities or make a living as journalists. Whether they write in English or Spanish, these individuals, as educators, journalists, and writers, promote an awareness and reaffirmation of Cuban literature and culture, as well as participate in shaping the culture of the United States. They have won national and international awards for their writing: Liz Balmaseda, a Cuban-American journalist, won a Pulitzer Prize in 1992; Pablo Medina and Silvia Curbelo both have won numerous literary awards, including National Endowment of the Arts fellowships and Cintas grants. Whether they live in Tampa or Miami, whether they write in English or Spanish, these writers share common threads in a giant tapestry that extends over more than two hundred years of literary production in Florida and touches at least two cultures.

From Felix Varela to Ricardo Pau-Llosa, Cuban writers in Florida have been driven by the need to explore the values of Cuban cultural identity, as well as the need to participate in a dialogue with the values of the host culture. In addition, many of these individuals have been active in promoting the literary arts in Florida through magazines, readings, awards, panels, and book fairs. The impact of their efforts transcends any specific culture.

There has indeed been a proliferation of Cuban writers in Florida since 1959. But their story is not a new one, for the history of Cuban literature is one of exile and displacement. It is a literature that evokes, from a distance, the concerns of its people and culture, concerns which also embrace their new home, in this case, Florida. Indeed, no study of Cuban history — or Florida and American history, for that matter — can be complete without an understanding of the relationship between these two places and the writers who served as their link.

WORKS CONSULTED

Boswell, Thomas D. and James R. Curtis. THE CUBAN AMERICAN
    EXPERIENCE: CULTURE, IMAGES & PERSPECTIVE. New Jersey: Rowman &
    Allanheld, 1984.

Caracciolo-Trejo, E. ed. PENGUIN BOOK OF LATIN AMERICAN VERSE.
    Middlesex: Penguin Books, 1971.

Carbonell y Rivero, José Manuel. EVOLUCION DE LA CULTURA CUBANA.
    La Habana: Imprenta "El Siglo XX," 1928.

Castellanos García, Gerardo. MOTIVOS DE CAYO HUESO: CONTRIBUCION A
    LA HISTORIA DE LAS EMIGRACIONES REVOLUCIONARIAS CUBANAS EN
    ESTADOS UNIDOS. Habana: Ucar, García y Cia, 1935.

Covington, James W. "Ybor City: A Cuban Enclave in Tampa." FLORIDA
    ANTHROPOLOGIST, Vol XIX, No. 2, (June 1966).

Cuza Malé, Belkis. EL CLAVEL Y LA ROSA: BIOGRAFIA DE JUANA BORRERO.
    Madrid: Ediciones Cultura Hispánica, 1984.

De la Vega, Garcilaso. LA FLORIDA DEL INCA. Madrid: Fundación
    Universitaria Española, 1982.

Estenger, Rafael. CIEN DE LAS MEJORES POESIAS CUBANAS. Miami:
    Mnemosyne Pub., 1969.

Fernández-Shaw, Carlos M. PRESENCIA ESPAÑOLA EN LOS ESTADOS UNIDOS.
    Madrid: Ediciones Cultura Hispánica, 1972.

Geiger, Maynard. BIOGRAPHICAL DICTIONARY OF FRANCISCANS IN SPANISH
    FLORIDA AND CUBA (1528-1841). New Jersey: St. Anthony Guild Press, 1940.

Grismer, Raymond and Manuel Rodríguez Saavedra. VIDA Y OBRA DE
    ESCRITORES CUBANOS. La Habana: Ediciones Alfa, 1940.

Isern, José. GOBERNADORES CUBANOS EN LA FLORIDA. Miami: AIP
    Publications Center, 1974.

——. PIONEROS CUBANOS EN U.S.A. Miami: Cenitt Press, 1971.

Jackson, Richard. BLACK WRITERS IN LATIN AMERICA. Albuquerque:
    University Of New Mexico Press, 1979.

Martínez, Julio A. ed. DICTIONARY OF TWENTIETH CENTURY CUBAN
    LITERATURE. New York: Greenwood Press, 1990.

Masud-Piloto, Felix Roberto. WITH OPEN ARMS: CUBAN MIGRATION TO
THE UNITED STATES. New Jersey: Rowman & Littlefield Publisher, 1988.

McCadden, Joseph & Helen. FELIX VARELA: TORCH BEARER FROM CUBA.
San Juan: Felix Varela Foundation, 1984.

Morell de Santa Cruz, Pedro Agustín. HISTORIA DE LA ISLA Y
CATEDRAL DE CUBA. La Habana: Academia de La Historia de Cuba,
Imprenta "Cuba Intelectual", 1929.

Mormino, Gary Ross. THE IMMIGRANT WORLD OF YBOR CITY: ITALIANS AND
THEIR LATIN NEIGHBORS IN TAMPA (1885-1985). Urbana: Univ. of
Illinois Press, 1987.

Pacheco, Ferdie. YBOR CITY CHRONICLE: A MEMOIR. Gainesville:
University Press of Florida, 1994.

Pérez Jr., Louis A. CUBA: BETWEEN REFORM AND REVOLUTION. N.Y.:
Oxford University Press, 1988.

Pérez Landa, Rufino. VIDA PUBLICA DE MARTIN MORUA DELGADO. La
Habana: Academia de la Historia, 1957.

Poyo, Gerald E. "Key West and the Cuban Ten Years War." FLORIDA
HISTORICAL QUARTERLY, 57 (January 1979).

——. "Cuban Revolutionaries and Monroe County Reconstruction Politics,
1868-1876." FLORIDA HISTORICAL QUARTERLY, 55 (April 1977).

Poyo, Raoul Alpizar. CAYO HUESO Y JOSE DOLORES POYO: DOS SIMBOLOS
PATRIOTAS. La Habana: Imprenta P. Fernández, 1947.

Ripoll, Carlos. CUBANOS EN LOS ESTADOS UNIDOS. New York: E. Torres & Sons: Las
Americas Publishing Co, 1987.

Rivero Muñiz, José. THE YBOR CITY STORY (1885-1954), Trans. Eustasio Fernández and
Henry Beltran, Tampa: n.p., 1976.

Ronning, C. Neale. JOSE MARTI AND THE EMIGRE COLONY IN KEY WEST.
New York: Praeger, 1990.

Tebeau, Charlton W. A HISTORY OF FLORIDA. Miami: University of Miami Press, 1971.

Tejera, Eduardo J. DIEGO VICENTE TEJERA. Madrid: Compañia de Impresores Reunidos, 1981.

Testé, Ismael, HISTORIA ECLESIASTICA DE CUBA. Barcelona: Artes Graficas,
Medianceli SA. 1974.

Westfall, L. Glenn. KEY WEST: CIGAR CITY U.S.A. Key West: Historic Key West
Preservation Board, 1984.

SELECTED PROSE AND
POETRY

FELIX VARELA

Felix Varela (1788–1853) is called the "Father of Cuban Nationalism," even though he spent most of his life abroad. Varela grew up and died in Florida more than a century ago. His writings, as well as his life, served and continue to serve as a beacon for other Cuban writers forced into exile. A journalist, a philosopher, a teacher, a theologian, a prominent member of the American Catholic Church, and a strong advocate of the poor, he was always loyal to his homeland and dedicated to his adopted land.

Felix Varela was born in Havana in 1788, son of the Spanish captain Francisco Varela. His mother, María Josefa, was Cuban. Orphaned by the age of six, he moved to Florida to live with his grandfather Don Bartolomé, who had been promoted to the rank of Brevet Colonel of the Third Battalion of Cubans garrisoned in St. Augustine. The Castle of San Marcos, then, became his childhood home.

The city was the capital of the Spanish colony, administered by Madrid through Havana. Varela was able to study in a school founded by Catholic missionaries under the tutelage of Father O'Reilly. When it was time for Varela to enlist in the military, he refused and chose the religious life instead. Don Bartolomé sent him to live with relatives in Havana to study at the Seminary of San Carlos.

He attended courses both at the Seminary and at the University of Havana. At nineteen, he received his Bachelor of Arts status and soon thereafter his Bachelor of Theology. He began his career as a teacher and writer at San Carlos. Three years later, he was ordained a priest by Bishop Espada. For the decade from 1812 to 1822, Felix Varela became Cuba's most respected and progressive philosopher and teacher. He added new fields of study, wrote textbooks, introduced the use of the vernacular in the classroom, and promoted the education of women. He personally initiated the first courses in modern science in Cuba.

Because of his reputation, he was chosen as spokesman in the Spanish Cortes. He unwillingly undertook this dangerous mission across the seas. In 1823, he offered a plan, recommended for adoption to the Cortes, for the virtual autonomy of Cuba and other overseas possessions. His plan included a constitution with a preamble and 189 articles dealing with rights, responsibilities, organization, and power of government. Varela tried to convince the Spaniards that it was better to be regarded as friends than as oppressors by the insurrectionists. He also proposed the abolition of slavery.

Many historians believe Cuba would have benefited much if Varela's plans had been adopted rather than ignored. He became disillusioned with Spain and convinced that nothing short of complete independence was necessary for the island. When the Cortes of 1823 found King Ferdinand inept and voted to depose him, Varela was one of three Cuban delegates to sign with the Spanish deputies.

The act was considered treason, and Varela could not return to Cuba. He escaped from Cadiz at night and eventually fled in exile to New York, where he continued to publish articles that advocated total freedom for Cuba.

In addition to his patriotic fervor, Varela was also a true man of the faith. During his stay in New York, he dedicated his entire life to the poor, especially the newly arrived Irish immigrants. He opened day schools for boys and girls and helped open a school for girls administered by the Sisters of Charity. He continued to write theological essays and became involved in controversies over anti-Catholic sentiments in New York and Philadelphia, sentiments that led to burnings of churches and to riots. He was concerned about the irreligiosity, fanaticism, and lack of tolerance he witnessed around him. As a consequence, he wrote the book of essays *Cartas a Elpidio*, an excerpt of which is included here.

Because of health reasons, Varela had to abandon his beloved parishioners in New York. He would spend his last six years in St. Augustine serving as a priest. Virtually abandoned by the Church in New York, he lived in Florida in a cell-like bare wooden room without his precious library. He died still in exile in 1853 at age sixty-four, almost blind, surrounded by humble parishioners of all ethnic backgrounds who considered him a saint. Throughout his life, he refused to return to Cuba while it remained subjugated to tyranny. He was buried in the Tolomato cemetery in St. Augustine, as he had requested. The Cubans soon built a shrine for his tomb.

In the early part of the twentieth century, Cubans had his remains removed to rest in Cuba, not without much controversy. The cemetery at Tolomato has been closed since 1890, and the chapel built by the Cubans in Florida rests unnoticed, untended, overgrown, and desolate in a quiet part of the city.

LETTERS TO ELPIDIO

Prologue

The *Letters to Elpidio* do not contain a defense of religion, although, by chance, in them are proven some of the dogmas of religion. My only objective has been, as the title makes clear, to consider irreligiosity, superstition, and fanaticism in their relation to the well-being of mankind, while reserving for another time the introduction of a polemical tract dealing with this important matter. I do not believe that I have offended any person in particular, but it has not been possible to avoid packing some punches in certain classes. I would have liked them to have been softer, but I am inclined to go overboard a bit, and so I hit hard.

Even though it could be said that each little tome forms a separate work, I have thought it prudent to present them as parts of one single work because of their relation to one another. Since my object is not to exasperate but to warn, the second and third volumes will remain unedited if by some misfortune the first is not well accepted; and, consequently, this one should be seen as a separate work.

I see that this *turkey* could gain me some enemies, but this is something to which I have become accustomed, since I have long been like the proverbial anvil — always under the hammer. I live very peacefully, however; as I wrote to a friend of mine, time and ill luck have battled long in my heart, until, convinced of the uselessness of their efforts, they have left me in peaceful possession of my long-standing and unwavering sentiments.

Irreligiosity Is the Source of Individual and Social Unhappiness

Time passes by, and people along with it, but perennial truth watches the course of their miserable race until they *precipitate* with hesitant steps into the abyss of eternity, leaving behind indelible signs of an existence by no power of their own. Yes . . . No doubt about it.

The unanimous voice issuing from the graves raises to heaven the sorrow-ful confession of human frailty, and the heavenly vaults send back to mortals a terrifying echo as a warning against daring enterprises and ill-fated ideas. This warning from the Divinity draws our attention to the underworld, where there lie love idols, hate objects, the spoils of war, and the ashes of the wise, the victims of wicked power and the powerful themselves. All of them, perpetually calm, warn the fools who walk over them that truth is formed in the highest, that it is one and immutable, holy and powerful, that it is the source of peace and the fountain of consolation, that it is found in the bosom of the Being with no begin-ning and cause of all beings.

The Existence of Evil

Those were my thoughts, my dear Elpidio, during some terrible times when my spirit, afflicted with the memories of those who were and now are no more, meditated about the regrettable history of human errors, about the sad conse-quences of unbridled passions, about the sufferings of virtue, which is always per-secuted, and about the victories of vice, which is always in power.

A survey of the annals of peoples throughout the centuries reveals the globe as a large field full of horror and death, where time has left a few monuments as eternal testimony to its power to destroy and to humiliate haughty mortals. But in the middle of such horrible ruins shine several beacons that have never been darkened by the shadows of death. These are, my dear Elpidio, the graves of the just, containing the relics of the temples of their souls, which flew to the center of truth, of the just who made love for truth the norm of their lives, and lived always in unity and peace under its influence.

Over the gravestones that cover up these tabernacles of virtue, imitators solve the great problem of happiness and look with compassion over those who, fascinated by miserable passion, chase after deceitful shadows and, deceived, become divided; once divided they hate themselves, once hated they destroy themselves.

Why, I have asked myself, why cannot clear ideas and noble examples attract all people to the true object of just love? Why do they not follow the majestic and evident road to happiness? Why is death spread abroad by the trustees of life? Why do those born to love now hate? Why does sorrow fill the faces which should glow with happiness? What are the regrettable causes that change the society of the children of the God of peace into immense hordes of ministers of anger?

These interesting questions soon found an answer. You can see stamped over the ruins of so many precious remains the footprints of three horrible monsters that caused their defeat and still run about sacrificing new victims. Take a look at insensitive irreligiosity, somber superstition, and cruel fanaticism, which travel along different paths but all tend to the same end — the destruction of the human race.

These monsters have been the constant object of my observations; I have tried to follow their footsteps, observe their attacks, watch their effects, and discover the means they employ to accomplish many atrocities. It is very clear that these most sorrowful meditations must have filled my soul with bitterness; and since friendship is the balm of affliction and the communication of ideas the relief for sensitive souls, allow me to entrust to you the feelings I have found within me and in a series of letters manifest to you the results of my research. Let us occupy ourselves, for the time being, with irreligiosity.

If experience did not prove that irreligious people do exist, reason could not prove that they could exist. When nature inspires love — and love is necessarily attracted to perfections more powerfully than steel to a magnet or celestial bodies are to the center of their circulation — how can a most perfect Being not attract the human will, and by what inexplicable anomaly can that will change the essence of goodness into an object of hate? . . .

Irreligiosity Destroys Hope and Leads To Despotism

The unhappiness that causes irreligiosity is followed, dear Elpidio, by the distrust of nations, a terrible evil which destroys all the plans of the wisest policy and annuls the efforts of the most just government. Once people are persuaded of the need of a guarantee against malice, and cannot find it in laws, which, as an old wise man said, are worthless without good customs, they cry out for a principle that produces and insures them. The life of the irreligious is an irrefutable testimony that they do not seek this coveted principle and that laxity is, almost always, joined by irreligiosity. How can they inspire faith? On their lips the sacred promise is a ridiculous fiction and a most insulting mockery. To swear by a God not believed in, or from whom nothing is expected and nothing feared, is to treat people as children, or as demented, whose ideas are usually heard only to humor and pacify them. Could there be a greater insult? Could one believe that those who begin by betraying a promise have the will to keep it? They present themselves as believers and swear as such, giving the impression that they have the same ideas and the same feelings, while in their minds they contradict each word, with the result that they do not believe each other nor does anyone believe them, no matter how well they play the role of comedian-politician.

The Destruction of Social Virtues

Once irreligiosity is spread throughout the social body, it destroys all links of appreciation, and, like poison, it corrupts and kills the body. Honor becomes a vain word; patriotism, a political mask; virtue, a fancy; and trust, a necessity. Do you think that I am exaggerating, Elpidio? Reflect on it and you will see that I am only copying. Yes, in the history of nations you will find the original of this image; you will see the political parties which, like heavy clouds driven by opposing winds, clash with fury, but incohesive they dissipate and disappear; or they may mix, forming new clouds which, driven by different winds, clash with distant ones causing the scene to repeat itself; and in this way they observe a dense veil that robs from our sight the luminous rays of the sun of justice. But, you will ask me, is irreligiosity always what forms the political parties? No, but it is always in all of them, without belonging to any, and corrupts them all. The irreligious just thinks of the moment, but the just considers eternity. Societies of the just have consistency, and societies of the perverse are frail. But when, unfortunately, such contrary elements as justice and irreligiosity come together, only a light impulse is enough to separate them; and once the action is interrupted, no matter how solid some of the parts may be, the whole dissolves. Here lies the pernicious effect of irreligiosity! . . .

An unbeliever lives only to enjoy this world as much as possible, and, according to his principles, he is foolish if, able to enjoy himself, he does not because of insignificant voices of virtue and honor; but, according to his own principles and those of a sound moral, even more foolish than he are those who are so naive as to believe what he says. The unbeliever is a beast chained by laws; but if its victim is within reach, or if the chains fail, destruction is certain. . . .

The Monster of Despotism

These masses, apparently so heterogeneous, convene perfectly in attracting crime and repelling virtue; and hence the result is that once the world is flooded by a deluge of evils, good people lose hope of purifying it and become discouraged. Their lack of action cleared the way for the ominous influence of tyranny, to which the perfidious, who pretended to be their enemies when they could not be their allies, soon offered their incense; and fatigued, the people yield to degrading despotism.

Do not think that I speak only of kings amongst whom there have been fathers of the nations and beasts that have anticipated the judgment. "Love your brother," St. John says, "and you will not suffer any scandal." "Why?" asks St. Augustine. "Because he who loves a brother tolerates everything in order to keep unity."

The harm would be less noticeable if the spirit who moved Bossuet's pen would move the hearts of the people who complain about the multitude of irreligious persons; but unfortunately it is noted that most of these grumbling persons want to find an object for their grumblings and they pretend to grumble even if they do not find it. There is hardly an illustrious person whom a multitude of *pious fanatics*, always in plenty, do not imagine as the worst irreligious person; and other *wily fanatics,* or assumed fanatics, do not calumniate in the most wicked way. These calumnies serve to plant a concern, innocent to a certain point, thanks to the religious persons' fear of the spread of irreligiosity; they do not realize that they sometimes get to such a point that they fail in justice by suspecting, or even believing without basis, that everybody is irreligious; and fail in charity, which asks not to consider them incurables until all of one's spiritual resources have been exhausted. These calumnies also bring about another effect that is even more disastrous, namely, that they lead irreligiosity into many persons who are far from it. This evil is very serious, because it is very senseless to create irreligious persons while you defend religion; and believe me, my dear Elpidio, that is very common and has deprived the sciences, the arts, and the whole of society of many useful members who have become harmful.

Social Tolerance

This type of tolerance is nothing more than a political consideration and as such it is only window dressing, and it is kept for no other purpose than to avoid upsetting the peace or making society unpleasant. People ridicule one another at the same time that they bestow a thousand courtesies on one another, and at times they declare vehemently that they see fit that each shall proceed as he may wish regarding religion and that everything practiced is good as long as the intention is good. There is no such thing, Elpidio; let us speak clearly: Generally this is a lie more detestable than any other, because it is the fruit of the most refined hypocrisy. Very few people indeed think this way because they have meditated on the subject or because they have a true indifference in matters of religion, which is equivalent to having no religion at all. Social religious tolerance never goes beyond being a measure of prudence, indicated by necessity and accompanied by compassion and, at times, by contempt towards those who profess another belief. Very few hold this attitude to the letter, and most keep it only when they cannot transgress it. Take a look at the facts, which is what is important.

History proves to us that nations, far from looking with kindness upon the enemies of their particular brand of worship, have persecuted them with more or less rage and cruelty, but always with much determination. Paganism shed the blood of Christians; heretics, for their part, have not been less cruel, and irreligiosity has far exceeded all of them. Overlooking many other eras, it would be enough for us to remember the times of Nero and Diocletian: the horrors and cruelties that the Aryans committed in the fourth century; the iconoclasts (or enemies of sacred images) in the eighth century under the protection of the emperors Leo the *Isauro* and his son Constantine *Copronimo;* and in the ninth century under the emperors Leo *Armenius,* Michael the *Beodus* and Teophilus; the excesses of the Lutherans because of the same hatred of images at the beginning of the sixteenth century, excesses that Luther himself condemned, spreading further the fanaticism of the new iconoclasts; the cruelties of the Anabaptists, not only against Catholics but against all the sects; the ravages caused by the Calvinists, who also burned people alive, and let servant serve as an example; the cruel persecutions indulged by the English people under the reigns of Henry VIII and the bloody Elizabeth; the atrocities of the Puritans and of the abominable Cromwell, and of the Puritans themselves in New England, which is to say, in the most educated part of this country, where the famous *Blue Laws* came to light, a copy of which I include.

In order to prove intolerance of irreligiosity it is enough to remember that in the French Revolution, to be recognized as a believer was enough to lose one's life. History offers us subsequent facts which confirm this assertion, but as you well know, Elpidio, it is not prudent to touch upon them. Let it be enough to observe that when the heretics or the irreligious cry out against the Inquisition, which never left Spain, Portugal, and Italy, and when they remind us of the history of France with its memorable *St. Bartholomew* or its cruel and treacherous massacre of Huguenots under the reign of Charles IX, they do so with the precise ignorance of their own history or with an unforgivable hypocrisy. It would be enough for them to observe that wise England has been the most infamous country as far as persecutions are concerned, for all others have given in to the struggles of the century, while that nation has given in only to *a point* simply because of the fear that has been inspired by the man of the century, the truly great man who, *without the aid of secret societies,* intrigue, or any weapon other than his tongue and his pen, has made the British power tremble. You are no doubt aware that I am talking about the modern Demosthenes, the incomparable O'Connell.

Anecdotes Showing the Lack of Social Tolerance Toward Catholics

As for this country, it is painful for me to admit that there is a legal but not social tolerance, at least as far as Catholics are concerned, for the sects keep each other in high regard. Let the facts speak for themselves, and since they are innumerable, let us consider a few of the more public ones. About four years ago a convent of Ursuline sisters was burnt down in Charlestown, a town near Boston, almost a suburb. The circumstances of this action are noteworthy. This convent, according to the nature of the institution, was a house of education. Located on a beautiful hill, it was inhabited not only by the sisters but by a great number of girls, most of them of Protestant, universalist, and unitarian parents. The sisters took great pains not to catechize their students nor to touch on points of religion that could compromise the good harmony they had with the parents, who were quite satisfied about the conduct of the nuns, and as proof of this kept their daughters in this establishment. However, the hatred towards Catholics in New England was such that at midnight a great multitude of people came over and set the convent on fire, causing sickness and even death among the sisters and the innocent girls, who were peacefully sleeping. Two days before, the newspapers had announced that this would be done, but it was regarded as unthinkable and no precautions were taken to avoid it.

The next day, articles started appearing in almost all the Protestant papers, condemning the cruel arsonists, and this *reshuffling in the papers* lasted for many months, reaching all parts of the United States. Many Catholics were beguiled, believing that Protestants truly felt that way and that they detested what had happened, but I have the pleasure of never having been taken in, for I abhor playing the role of the deceived one. I did not look behind the scenes and I only read the newspapers. I told a friend of mine, "these people [are] bestowing compliments on us in the newspapers so that we may become careless, as well as to avoid the opprobrium that their actions would cause them, but they shall repeat it very soon." I did not deceive myself, Elpidio; time has proven that it was not a mere suspicion of mine. Now they say that the sisters are returning to Boston and that they expect that the public treasury will compensate the losses they suffered, for there is a new law that provides for such cases, but I suspect that their case will be declared an exception for being a Catholic institution.

This experience proves, my Elpidio, that the public opinion in the city of Boston was against the Catholic religion. The city is very far from the tolerance that is spoken about so much, but practiced so little. A fire always evokes compassion, and especially when it is accompanied by such circumstances as I have just related; but the Bostonians limited themselves to the *lamentations they published in the newspapers* and they did not believe that they should do anything for an educational institution that was reduced to ashes on account of religious hatred. This very fact proved the extent of this hate. Even the few who truly desired to build the academy again so that their daughters could receive a select education did not dare take up a public collection, for they knew full well what the public opinion towards Catholics was.

This is a country in which each one is free to believe and to do as one wishes on religious matters; it is thus even more noteworthy that public opinion, and public opinion alone, should close the doors to charity, justice, and the common good. I shall say even more: Not even Catholics were exhorted to proceed without fear in rebuilding their academy, and everything was limited to charges against the arsonists, as it was in earlier times against the thieves of the *Sierra Morena;* but without making sure that the unfortunate one who dared to go through would not be taking too many risks. If the Bostonians truly had the spirit of universal tolerance, when they saw that this philanthropic principle was attacked by such an unpleasant public gesture, they would have taken the opportunity to consolidate their doctrine, extending a charitable hand to those Catholics who had so unjustly been persecuted; but undoubtedly the religious principle that directs their conscience was stronger and they were not able to bring themselves to protect a few nuns from a Catholic institution. Do you think that I blame them? No, my friend. I shall always bemoan their blind obstinacy, but as long as they are blind, I am not amazed that they should behave in such a manner, and even though they do evil when they burn and destroy, they act rightly for following their conscience and thus not supporting the extension of a religion that in fact they detest. My dear Elpidio, I detest only their abominable hypocrisy in feigning that they have a tolerance when in reality they do not.

The funniest thing about all of this was the judicial process undertaken against the arsonists. In a country like this, in which everything is thoroughly investigated and a criminal never escapes, no one was able to find out anything whatsoever about this fire. Only a thirteen- or fourteen-year-old boy was found guilty. They really knew that because of his young age he would come out all right. Even the Catholics themselves took steps so that he would be set free. All others who had been arrested *were found innocent.* . . .

While I was staying in Boston there was another case which could have had deadly consequences had the bishop not proceeded with his usual prudence. On the feast of Pentecost, just before the principal mass, a good number of people were in and around the doors of the church waiting for the festivities to begin, when someone in the house across the street threw a cross tied with a rope out of a window and jingled it up and down in various ways. When the Catholics became aware of the mockery, they went in and asked the bishop what they should do; he told them, "venerate that *cross* that they throw out of a window no matter how they try to profane it, and beg them to use all of their influence so that a cross may be placed in every door of every house in Boston." Thanks to this prudent advice the Catholics were peaceful, who had been ready to enter that house and scare the sacrilegious jokers out of their wits.

Two or three years after the fire at the Ursuline convent in Charlestown, when the enemies of the Catholic religion realized how well they had fared in their scandalous deed, they wished to perpetrate another in this city of New York by burning our cathedral church. In order to prepare the people for such an attempt, Protestant ministers began to preach almost daily that Catholics would like to submit this country to the Pope and that we had set up the Inquisition, whose dungeons were ready under our cathedral church. No matter how absurd their assertions were, they were believed, because of the Protestants' desire to find a motive to attack us. The burning of our church was certainly agreed upon; and since projects of this nature require purely executing hands, which can always be found among those of limited education, it seems that they made use of the butchers, among whom I do not know if there is a single Catholic. They were not too careful and they had a conversation in public at the market, which was over-heard by one of the merchants who was a Catholic and who immediately came to tell me, for she belonged to our congregation. Under other circumstances I would not have paid any attention, but as I remembered what had happened in Boston and knowing how public opinion was being stirred up against Catholics as a result of the *charitable* sermons of their ministers, I put the *trustees* or administrators of the cathedral church on guard. They informed our people very soon by word of mouth because, being lay people, they were in touch with our people.

On the night we feared that the attack would take place, more than five hundred Catholics gathered around the cathedral church. The governor of the city immediately came over, either because he was told what was going on or because the unexpected large number of Catholics around a closed church caught his attention. Two or three hundred would-be arsonists came at the appointed time. But imagine their surprise when they turned the corner and saw our church surrounded by so many people! The Catholics immediately sent someone to tell the attackers they should leave, because for their part they were determined to defend their property. This information, or the news that the governor of the city would take whatever measure was necessary against them, made them retreat and go away. The Catholics were afraid that they would come back and they were determined to spend the entire night around the cathedral. The governor of the city then told Reverend Thomas Levins, a Catholic priest (who was a curate of the very cathedral), that he should address the Catholics in a high spot assuring them that the government would be responsible for paying for anything that was destroyed by the people, but that they should not be afraid of this taking place because the police would break up any disorder. Reverend Levins did as requested, and the Catholics went away immediately.

Last year in the city of Baltimore they made another attempt to attack a convent of the Carmelite sisters (which, if I am not mistaken, is the only one of that order in this country), but it did not have any serious consequences, although they had the barbaric pleasure of upsetting those poor sisters. It must be said, however, that in the states of the south there is not as much animosity against us as in those of the north; and especially in Maryland they are very kind towards us, perhaps because of the memory of Lord Baltimore, who was a Catholic and from whom the principal city takes its name; and of the illustrious Carroll, who was one of the signers of the Declaration of Independence of this country and the last of the signers to die. His family is quite revered and respected and has great influence in that state. Bishop Carroll, the first Archbishop of Baltimore, also belongs to this family. . . .

Translated by Felipe J. Estevez.

DIEGO VICENTE TEJERA

Diego Vicente Tejera (1848–1903) was known primarily as a poet, but he was also a short-fiction writer, orator, and political activist. He was born in Santiago in 1848, and lived through a very turbulent time in Cuba. He spent most of his adult life in exile.

Until he was sixteen years old, he studied at the Seminary of Santiago. His father then sent him to New York to continue his studies. From there, he moved to Caracas, Venezuela, finished high school, and began to study medicine. These plans were interrupted when he was arrested for his revolutionary activities against President Guzmán Blanco. He was saved by the family of his friend Amelia (the recipient of his love in his most famous poem, "The Hammock," included here). From Venezuela, he ended up in Barcelona and eventually back in the United States.

While in Key West, he participated in revolutionary activities, translated major literary works into Spanish, and directed a newspaper. Tejera's mastery as an orator was important in keeping Martí's pro-independence fervor alive after Martí's death. He frequently lectured on a variety of issues at the San Carlos Institute in Key West. Topics included racism, women, education, and socialism. We have included excerpts from one of these lectures. He was a strong presence in the exile community on the key at the end of the nineteenth century.

Tejera later emigrated to Paris and Madrid and finally returned to Cuba, where he started the Cuban Socialist Party and the Labor party in 1901. He also continued his involvement with newspapers and magazines until his death in 1903.

IN THE HAMMOCK

*I*n the hammock, existence,
sweetly, swaying,
slips away.
Perhaps to blame my affliction,
my voice its gentle powers
venerates.

Let the sultan enjoy in repose
the infinite pleasures
of the harem,
and in voluptuous ecstasy
feign, among his women,
an Eden.

I do not envy his
fabulous land, nor his radiant
blue sky,
nor the artistries that the
dazzling seraglio of Istanbul
embraces.

And I do not covet his power,
nor do I fear when his rage
explodes,
and he humiliates, from his throne,
the village that trembles in silence
from dread . . .

My sun is so vivid,
my tropical ground so
splendid,
and in my rustic shack
the provident sky
offers me such fortune

that if the Turk would surprise
the enchantments of my
dark life,
his empire, immediately, would give me
only one day to be pleased
with my fortune!

Upon a picturesque hill
in the center of a lush
farm,
where among the plantain trees
emanates a fresh, clean, babbling
spring;

poorly constructed,
far from man, among seas
of green,
where only the murmur
of tropical trees and palm groves
sounds at my ear,

rises its rough wall
this home, where in a delicious
languor,
I hurry to enjoy such joys
that I dare covet
no more.

How pleasant it is to live in peace
with oneself, without sorrows
making us moan,
and in my world, my soul absorbed,
perceiving barely
the course of time!

Oh, from the treble, the soft echo
of love feigned exhaling

anguishes
or growing sleepy listening to
the zephyr, among the leaves,
whispering.

What does it matter to me that an opulent
monarch should buy or not buy
false caresses,
if in the placid isolation
of my hut I have
a thousand delights?

Here, full of my sorrows,
the breeze placates the heat
without ceasing,
and I, stretched on the sand,
can watch
my small farm, without shame.

Or I can forget the farm
and be happy,
having already calmed the tender moan
of my turtledoves with grains
of corn.

Having already sucked the juice from
the pineapples, or from the sugarcane
its honey,
having inhaled the smoke from the tobacco
or the delightful essence
of the coffee.

Or I sleep to the slow swaying
of the hammock, or I amuse myself
contemplating
how, at the whim of the wind,
the canefield ripples
like a sea.

Or I surprise the small bird
building
his nest in the aged tropical tree,
or I admire the hummingbirds
hovering over
the rose.

Or the image of the
only being that reigns over me
delights me,
Amelia, my glory,
olive-skinned, more bewitching
than an houri.

Happy is one, who, with fascination,
dreams with sweet stories
of love,
and sleeps by the kiss
of breezes, by the murmur
of sugarcane!

Disdain the backwater and take care of
overcoming the mundane
surf
he who, by his disgrace, forgets
that our earthly voyage is
so short.

I, who notice how one crosses
the sea in a hurry, shall
barely row,
and at the blowing of a soft breeze,
by waters always serene,
shall sail.

Let the sun's rays respect my roof;
the fresh rain nurture
my ground;
I shall live within the breast
of Amelia; her beauty
with love overflows.
Let the forest howl, the river sound,
displaying all its April
finery;
a thousand dreams
will sway me in my shack
and snatch me in their wings . . .
And the lies of the world
will never disturb my sweet
repose,
and in my retreat
I shall always be happier
than a sultan!

Translated by Carolina Hospital.

DIEGO VICENTE TEJERA

EDUCATION IN DEMOCRATIC SOCIETIES

The course that I want to follow for these humble conferences demands that I consider today the type of education provided in our society in order to see if it is appropriate for a new democratic people . . . for a people without traditions, a people unconcerned, a bit frivolous, a bit vain, a bit finicky, with a vivid imagination and strong passions; but with a natural kindness and a clear intelligence.

It is a delicate topic which should be studied by all our scholars. I will only be able to scratch the surface, but we should begin to call attention to this topic so that as we reshape other aspects of our culture, we also consider education in a new way.

Indeed, it would not be a waste of time to speak a bit, first, about what education unfortunately means to the popular classes and what it should mean instead. Indeed, education establishes differences between individuals, differences which can injure those who feel inferior even though these differences may be purely social and to a certain extent legitimate. If education were what it should be morally, social differences would hardly be noticeable and would not be so shameful for anyone. If education would in truth improve individuals, then its first effect would be to make people kinder, and disinclined to demonstrate superiority in their treatment of those who had not been educated to the same extent. True education would even out the rough edges in people's characters, and leave only smooth polished surfaces, so that in forced daily social dealings there would not be scrapes nor conflicts, but rather peaceful encounters. Given that, I would not hesitate in calling anyone — even if such a person had university degrees, wore elegant suits, and were full of delicacies and politeness in social gatherings — a spoiled brat, if this person behaved with snobbery and superiority in the presence of another whom they considered inferior.

Unfortunately, individuals such as these, of both genders, abound in our society, and that is the first reason I have for suspecting that our education is bad. They abound, I say, and we can blame them for the negative attitudes the

Excerpts from a speech given at the San Carlos Institute
in Key West, October 17, 1887.

popular classes have against the so-called cultured ones. These ignorant people are making education disagreeable, by giving it unheard-of airs; proof that they confuse — the most awkward ones — dignity with haughtiness and natural advancement with phony loftiness. They don't realize that from the moment they commit their first vulgarity, just one, they deserve the name of vulgarian, which means uneducated. And they fall, as a matter of fact, to a lower level than those they wish to scorn. . . .

Good moral and intellectual education are not only desirable, but necessary in democratic societies. The direction and government of our things must be entrusted to all, and if the responsibility were to rest more on one class than another, it would be on the working class. Because of its numbers, it would have more weight on the general decisions.

But education for public life must rest on private education, which begins with the parents before the infant even opens its eyes: the citizen must leave the home already formed. And it is here, before the spectacle I witness in our future free homeland, where suddenly I see our present education with all its deformity and deficiency. The brutal Spanish regime, to which we have been subjected, has not prepared us, has not been able to prepare us for the exercise of freedom and human rights, nor has it allowed us to acquire great domestic virtues. By distancing us from business affairs, it has made us become indifferent to them. Furthermore, they have corrupted our customs with their example of immorality always triumphant, thus obscuring the clarity of our principles; and I haven't spoken of how they have purposely and maliciously perverted us, creating and fostering vices which we will carry with us for a long time.

Thus, we have to proceed, without any delay, with implementing the total education of the individual as well as the citizen. Because it is impossible, from every which way, given our inclinations and limitations, to enter our new life without stirring it up, perhaps forever. We are still *colonos* in character, and if we do not transform ourselves, we risk the danger of not knowing what else to do except repeat the dreadful pattern of the old colony. . . .

In any case, we should begin to fulfill the new responsibilities imposed by our new circumstances, instilling as soon as possible in our families the principles of a rational education to substitute the insincere education received during colonial times.

Was it insincere, yes? Didn't they educate us only for private life? Was it not the attitude that the ultimate purpose of education was to shine in social gatherings? The poor instruction we were given, was it not generally classic and for adornment? Didn't we maintain a rancid preoccupation with caste, affirming that in society two types of individuals exist, those that are our equal and those that are inferior, and the first should be treated with consideration and the latter with disdain, so as to keep them at a distance? Was it not repeated time after time that work in itself was denigrating, acceptable only of necessity and, given this, that careers providing benefits and fame should be chosen, and manual rugged occupations should be left for the lower classes? Were we not taught to spend money on objects of vanity and to put on airs, whether we were rich or not? Was it not considered in good favor to drink, play, engage in duels, dress well without paying the tailor, and publicly and verbally dishonor women? Was disgusting gossip and idle chatter not promoted in every home, these vices which have turned our society, which is at heart good and generous, into a seething commotion of ill-will? Did we not talk about the pillages of the bandit in the countryside and the robberies of the government employee and the commercial smuggler in the city as witty accomplishments? Was it not general practice to mock the laws, and especially to violate, *de guapo*, police mandates? . . .

Well, now, we should do exactly the opposite; we have to educate ourselves for a serious and honorable social life and for a public life raised against difficulties and dangers; we should educate ourselves not to be dandies at social gatherings, but rather men on whose actions depend the success or failure of their country. We should be educated to respect all our citizens, treating them all with equal consideration, and treating with even greater consideration those who are weaker and less fortunate. We should be educated in work, seeing it as a blessing, not only because it develops the national wealth, but because it allows the children of the popular classes to reach, in a safe and decorous way, the level of classes privileged in other ways. We should be educated in an austere economy that creates fortunes and is proof of morality in the one who practices it; it will allow us, with the fruit of our labor, all the legitimate satisfactions accorded, while absolutely shunning those of mere vanity, the most costly and impure, the most unworthy of a true democracy. We should be educated in studies, providing nourishment for the spirit, redeeming us from the slavery of ignorance and furnishing us with the rewards that science and art can offer us. We should be educated in the exercise of strict virtues that ennoble and preserve a republic, rejecting vice, as appealing as it may seem, censuring those that are irresponsible, as well as those that offend women. We should be educated in charity and goodwill, eliminating in the home the first sign of ill-will or neighborhood gossip that may creep in, because respect for others is the best safeguard to self-respect and because the pleasure of insulting others can lead to gratuitous injury, the pleasure of the wicked, which would reveal the end of kindness in our society. We should be educated to defend the needs of the community in which we live, considering our enemies those who steal whether in the countryside or in the city. We should be educated in a profound respect for the law and the precepts of our community, which are the expression of our will and without which a society cannot endure. We should learn that fortunes are acquired only through our own intelligence and effort, abandoning gambling, a practice which takes more than gives and which destroys the entire point of education, which is to dignify and enrich, while this vice impoverishes and degrades. In sum, we should be educated to look at ourselves and others scrupulously, to keep our cities, our homes, and ourselves physically and morally clean, and to shun anything that might contaminate the body or poison the soul. . . .

No man should enter social life without possessing the sum of knowledge not only useful but necessary to think critically and independently. That sum of knowledge, those notions of natural and political science, of philosophy and history, could form a compulsory program of education in Cuba and would be the indispensable degree for entering the career of life. The classic degree, the old degree, was not appropriate, since it was a pedantic construct of inconsistent and foolish topics. . . .

I believe that our current education is detestable; I believe that a large part of our so-called cultured class should abandon unjustified pretensions to a distinguished origin and lose those false aristocratic airs, so unbecoming, thus assuming to the fullest the democratic spirit, which, by the way, does not exclude social distinction based on virtue, courteous behavior, and proper manners. I believe our culture should completely renovate its education, fixing defects belonging to its race and vices acquired under the terrible Spanish domination; I believe this moral education should be accompanied by intellectual education, providing now, as a free people, an intellectual level high enough to be able to practice with discretion political sovereignty and to prevent the rise of an oligarchy among us. You can see that the problem has a simple exposition, which leads us to assume its resolution can also be easy. I judge it so, and I expect the most from my people, who, in spite of their defects and vices, possess solid natural virtue. Foreigners are beginning to recognize them; already an important America admires the way the Cuban people have carried out their long immigration, struggling well in a disadvantageous environment, maintaining themselves with decorum because of their untiring labor, their temperate tastes, and the moderation of their customs, not contributing to the statistics of crime by foreigners in this vast country. Reason for pride and hope. These immigrants will take back to their homeland the habits acquired in this great school of democracy. . . .

Translated by Carolina Hospital.

JOSE MARTI

*J*osé Martí (1853–1895) was the most important Cuban literary and political figure of the nineteenth century. He was dedicated to the liberation of Cuba from Spanish rule and was politically active his entire life. He also found time to be a prolific writer. He wrote essays on a diversity of subjects including racism, Walt Whitman, America, art exhibits, and political philosophy. He also produced several collections of poetry, most importantly *Ismaelillo, Simple Lyrics*, and *Complex Poems*. The sculptured simplicity, yet subtle tension and insight of his poetry, especially in his *Simple Lyrics*, made a profound change in the approach to poetry in Latin America, change referred to as Modernism. In addition, his verses have become internationally known, often recited, and even borrowed for folk songs and ballads. He also wrote a play, a novel, a political pamphlet, and numerous articles for newspapers. Undoubtedly, Martí's literary works revitalized Latin American literature and opened the way for a new autonomous voice.

Martí was born in Havana to Spanish parents of limited means. Rafael de Mendive became his patron and sent him to the Institute of Havana to study. At fifteen, he founded a newspaper with Mendive, *The Free Fatherland*, which cost him his freedom. At that young age, he was imprisoned and later exiled to Spain where he eventually received a law degree. While in Spain, he published a pamphlet: *The Political Prisons in Cuba*. After failing to have an impact in Spain, he decided to return to Cuba. On his journey back, he traveled to Paris, Mexico, and Guatemala. In Cuba, he was imprisoned and exiled once more. This time he found residency in the United States where he stayed for fifteen years.

While in the United States, Martí wrote steadfastly, while also giving speeches and conducting conferences in his travels throughout the U.S. and Latin America, looking for support for Cuban independence. He became the intellectual guide for the movement and was chosen leader of the Cuban Revolutionary

Party, in Key West, in 1892. Martí traveled extensively to Florida, residing for long periods of time in Tampa, Key West, and Jacksonville — so much so that he became an intrinsic figure for the Cuban communities in Florida. He would speak eloquently to audiences of thousands, seeking spiritual, political, military, and financial support for Cuba's independence. The communities in Florida gave him enthusiastic support and eventually became the backbone of the independence movement. The speeches he gave in these Florida cities became famous and part of his literary canon; one is included here, "Los pinos nuevos," which was inspired by the Florida landscape and proclaimed at the Liceo Cubano of Tampa in 1891.

Unfortunately, instead of remaining in exile, supporting the campaign from abroad, Martí decided to join the first revolutionaries to land on the island in 1985. He was killed that same year in Dos Ríos. Because of his tragic death at a relatively young age, his devotion to his homeland, and his masterful literary talents, Martí has become a martyr and an almost mythical figure in the Cuban and Latin American psyche.

THE NEW PINES

Cubans

The night inspires a respectful silence rather than words: Let the flower of resurrection that grows over the grave be the language of the dead. Occasional tears and hymns of mourning are not the proper tributes for those who, with the light of their death, enlightened an indifferent world to the empire of abomination and greed. Those funeral wreaths are here out of respect, not out of death; those flags may beat half mast, but not our hearts. I come before you after a busy creative day, and I have asked my mind to mourn so that I may console you with my words, but my mind will not mourn. Yesterday I felt break at the foot of this podium the waves of real anger that came cresting from our land. But today I do not feel them, nor do I hear any weeping, or see supplicant hands or listeners with bowed heads. No! What I see before me are heads held high, and outside this packed hall come waves of people marching. And so the sun on the clear horizon raises its golden chalice over the shadows of night.

Let others bemoan the purposeful death: I believe in it as I believe in the pillow, the leavening, and the triumph of life. The morning after the storm the earth spills forth a fountain of freshness from the hole left by an uprooted tree; the green of the forest is brighter, the air unfurls like a flag, the sky is a canopy of blue glory, and the hearts of men are flooded by an immense joy. There, over the deposits of death, a light flaps its wings surging out of decay, as if redeeming itself, and disappears in the depths of the sky. The reddest, lightest poppy grows over unkempt graves. The tree that gives the best fruit is the one with a dead man under it.

Let others lament the death that served to free the fatherland from a forced complicity with crime. Such a death is the fuel that fires the commitment of our souls and tempers them for posterity. Virtue rises immortal from the cemetery like morning fog; it garlands a timid earth; it lashes lowly faces; it saturates the air; it enters triumphant into the hearts of the living. Death gives us leaders; death gives

A speech given November 27, 1891, at the *Liceo Cubano*
of Tampa in commemoration of the students executed on
November 27, 1871.

us lessons and examples; death guides our index finger over the book of life. And so, the spirit of our country is being woven from these continuous but unseen threads.

Our words must do more than describe a list of horrors. We will not humiliate those who have repented in order to condemn those who have not. Nor shall the martyr's tomb turn into a fighting arena. And it will not be said, even in the blind midst of battle, what it is that moves the hearts of men to ferocity and rancor. It is not in the Cuban character, nor will it ever be, to steep itself in blood to the waist and to remind the world of its crimes with a mound of dead children; it is not in the Cuban character to live, like the jackal in its cage, always going in circles around hatred! Let us speak here of the profound and sacred love that we have for those youngsters whom decorum raised suddenly to the greatest heights. They were sacrificed in order to advertise to a world ever indifferent to our cry the fully just way in which the earth stood up against its masters. Let us salute with deep-felt gratitude those who, at the first call of death, rose smiling from the comfort and security of common life to serve as models of heroism. They stand as mysterious symbols of patriotic strength and of the hidden but certain power of the Creole spirit.

And who was at the head of the sacrificial procession when death's drum sounded and the wave of weeping crested and the murderers lowered their heads? Who was the first one, smiling peacefully, walking firmly, so young enlightened? He was a fine and selfless Creole with down on his chin and a bird in his soul, who used to bounce like a spark up and down the halls of the school. He wore rings on his fingers, and his feet were like jewels: He was all good taste and delicacy and carriage, not a wrinkle in his airy thoughts. Now he marched firmly, leading the procession, that mischievous, feather-brained boy of the breezy classrooms, with his hands full of rings and his foot like a jewel! And the other one, the quiet one, whom his mates thought to be dull and slow? His fallen face filled with a special beauty, and his patriotic soul grew with righteous power. Before he went out to greet death, he embraced his friends strongly and he shook their hands calmly and inspired their tears! And so, in the coming struggles glory shall rise triumphant from the darkest breast! And so, the armies of tomorrow shall rise from our hidden valor! And so, when the moment comes, the indifferent and guilty ones of today, the vain and careless ones of today, shall be forced to compete in battle with the most valiant ones. The sixteen-year-old boy walked ahead, smiling with a special glow, looking behind him lest one of his companions fall out. . . .

And shall I speak of the brutal prison and its horrible collection of vices – fish and wine for the general's table, a course for every crime? Old folk were knifed for pure enjoyment – old folk who gave their country thirteen strong men – so that their suffering would not be in vain. Dying prisoners were turned over on the ground at the point of a saber to see if they could be revived. Torturers did their work while a marching band played so that the screams of the broken victims could not be heard beyond the stone walls. Well, these are crueler horrors, and sadder and more useless, and more to be feared than that of walking barefoot! Or shall I recall the cold dawn when the surviving students, afoot while the rest of Madrid slept, went about the city nailing to the doors of palaces and under the crosses of churches reports of the crime and the national shame that appalled the waking city? Or shall I recall a day, a summer day in Madrid, when at the heels of a dry and livid man, with sparse beard and soul, very twilled, renowned, and pompous, came a sickly child, held by a hand barely stronger than his, yelling at the awful greed monger: "Scoundrel! Blackguard!" I will remember instead the magnanimous Spaniard, beloved guest at all of our homes, honored here symbolically next to the heroic avengers. Facing the mouth of death itself, this man preferred the poverty of justice to the rewards of complicity and refused to join the murder with his sword! They say that he is gnawed by regret in a corner where the wrath of the powerful conqueror cannot console him and that he willingly accepts the affections of the conquered. Let the mercy of our grateful Cuban flowers fall on all good Spaniards!

All that remains of our land in the aftermath are the four skeletons resting from south to north, over the other four that rest from north to south; all that remains is a cuff link next to a dried-out hand and a mound of bones embracing in the depths of a lead box! Cuba will never forget, nor will those who know of heroism forget, the man who, disregarding all danger, raised his hand and stopped the coffin that became the country's fountainhead of blood: He descended into the earth with his loving hands, and, at the bitter hour, the sort of moment that suddenly joins man to eternity, he touched icy death and bathed the skulls of his mates with his weeping! The sun shined in the sky when he raised in his arms the venerated bones out of the grave: Sunlight will always fall on the avenger who acts without hatred!

The fatherland is purer and more beautiful because of the death of those young men. Stop then the lamentations that are best reserved for a useless death. Countries thrive on heroic leavening. Great heroism will cure great crime. Where there was much evil, let there be much greatness. Magnificent laws run invisibly through life. These men died at the hands of the inhumanity and greed that tormented their country. The world shook with the poetry of their youth and the candor of their innocence. With undeniable logic and reason, they emboldened the spirit of those who doubt the determination and virtue of a people in appearance indifferent and frivolous. They left the classroom laughing carelessly, or thinking of a girlfriend or a dance, and entered firmly, without a knee buckling or a hand trembling, into a barbaric death. Our two peoples shall inevitably come either to a just agreement or a violent extermination. In order to unite us with the respect that remorse imposes on some and the pity that those who feel remorse inspire in others, the merciful avenger rose, thereby assuring the work of justice through the triumph of moderation. Tomorrow, as today they do in exile, the brothers and sisters of the victims, and those who, placing honor above the accidents of birth, do not want to call themselves brothers and sisters of the murderers, shall go to place flowers in a free land at the altar of forgiveness.

Today let us sing the hymn of life before the memorial of their graves. Yesterday I heard it coming from the earth itself, when we came to this gracious town. The landscape was damp and shadowy; the streams ran turbulent and muddy; the sugarcane, sparse and withered, did not move sorrowfully like the one far away that seeks redemption for those who nourished it with their death. Rather, its blades entered, rough and sharp, like daggers through the heart. In defiance of the storm and clouds, one pine stood with its top raised. Suddenly the sun broke through a clearing in the forest, and there in the midst of the shimmering light, I saw growing over the yellowed grass, next to the blackened trunks of fallen pines, bunches of new pines. That is what we are: The new pines!

Translated by Pablo Medina.

from SIMPLE LYRICS

XXIII

I want to leave this world
by its natural door:
to die they must take me
in a cart of bright green leaves.

Do not put me in the dark
to die as a damned traitor
I am a man and as a man
I shall die facing the sun.

XXXIX

I grow a white rose
in January as in July
for the friend free of lies
who an honest hand shows.

And for the cruel soul
who tears out this heart with which I live
grubs nor thistles do I grow,
I grow a white rose to give.

Translated by Carolina Hospital.

MARTIN MORUA DELGADO

*M*artín Morúa Delgado (1856–1910) was a prominent political and literary figure. He was held in high esteem in Cuba for his role as a revolutionary, as well as for being a strong proponent of the integration of blacks into Cuban culture. Himself the son of slaves, Morúa proposed outlawing political parties based on race, an action designed to force blacks to work within the system. The Ley Morúa, though well intentioned, was used after Morúa's death to justify the massacre of thousands of blacks involved in an uprising in 1912 and to undermine black consciousness in a post-abolitionist Cuba.

Morúa began his literary and political career as a journalist in 1878. In 1879, he began the newspaper *El Pueblo* in Matanzas, and dedicated it to black consciousness. In 1880, he left the island for the States. A year later, he published in Key West a collection of essays which he sent back to Cuba to sell for a small amount. To make ends meet, he became a reader in a cigar factory, the first black man to do so. During his ten-year residence in Key West, he made periodic visits to New York. He also started the magazine *Revista Popular*, learned English, and translated many works into Spanish, including the popular novel *Called Back* by Hugh Conway, while continuing his revolutionary activities. We have included excerpts from two of the many articles he published while living in exile.

Back in Cuba, Morúa wrote the two novels that would situate him further as a significant literary figure: *Sofía* and *La Familia Unzuazu*. In both of these naturalist, antislavery novels, he explored the social and psychological effects of slavery on the individual, even after the abolition of the institution. He also wrote numerous essays of literary criticism.

At the beginning of the war of independence, Morúa Delgado returned to exile and settled in Tampa. He made a living once more as a reader at a cigar factory and continued his revolutionary involvement. Eventually, he joined the insurgents on the island. After the war, he became well known as a political orator, especially during his eight years as a senator. In 1909, he even rose to become the president of the Senate, the last black man to hold that high office in Cuba. He died in 1910, while serving the government as Minister of Agriculture.

DUTY CALLS

Throughout the endless chatter of this great metropolis, great benefactor of the free world, exemplary monument of the destiny of America; throughout the imperturbable movement of progress, which with its hundreds of arms seems to thrust us everywhere into betterment, towards modern civilization; throughout all this, so grand and so magnificent, a weak voice resounds, with the incessant power, with the severe decadence of the invincible spirit, of that immortal being who thrusts a painful scream, which coming from the depth of his soul penetrates that of every worthy Cuban. With a sad lament, it shows him the way to responsibility, bringing him back from any distraction any circumstance could have taken him.

That sad voice, painful, but also affectionate and moving, like the impressive supplication of a great being, that is the voice of our homeland.

Yes, our homeland cries in pain because of the abandonment of its derailed children.

It calls for help, exhausted by its servitude. Greed, exploitation, infamy, all that is criminal, all that is unheard of, assaults it, tires it, weakens it until it loses all its vitality.

In that situation, from whom better to ask for help? From whom else could it hope to receive support, in these moments of crisis, when it has been broken?

Cuba, beautiful Cuba, ascends in the life of its people with the deplorable ascent of the slave who produces.

Cuba used to be . . . looked at from a certain point of view. It was considered merely a place where you send a new steward to increase the productivity of its workers, to polish the axles in his machinery, to oil and clean the springs so the wheels and the fan belts run better, without abandoning completely the valves that will destroy in an impulse his magnificent armament.

Later, it was finally a colony. It had ascended. It was special. As such it had to follow special laws.

An article published in 1888, while Morúa Delgado was residing in Key West, from the New York newspaper *El Separatista*.

But Cuba was dissatisfied. It saw among its people certain "blue bloods" imitating European nobility, dressed in the degrading attire of the serfs of medieval times.

Cuba was more receptive to the enlightenment than Spain. Cuba had enlightened itself. While, in Spain, travelers still used caravans and the courts regarded the railroad as absurd, here the locomotive whistled, amusing the worker at his task; and while the civilized took to the sea in interminable sailing journeys, the uncivilized plowed the blue waters with the latest techniques introduced by the American civilization. Furthermore, didn't Cuba speak in its Athenian courts? Didn't it write in its newspapers? Didn't it philosophize in its books? Didn't it analyze in its sciences? Yes, education had exalted itself. Cuba belonged to the enlightenment.

It considered itself large and others considered it small.

And from that attitude, grounded in its isolated servitude, it decided to prove to its tyrants, to the entire world, that it deserved the respect of other enlightened nations, and it rose against the miserable condition it was subjected to. Its decision was unjust; as much unjust as severe, so severe, it obtained the respect even of its oppressors and was considered a province.

But always dependent.

More or less, always a slave. Thus it remains, thus it is maintained.

And from this abject condition, as a slave admired by its master, with all the perverse adulation of the exploiter, it has expended its strength to leave.

Cuba weakens but does not despair. It trusts its people, and trusts with reason, because it has never been abandoned by the competent.

Rome freed itself from the chains that oppressed it. It obtained more than it counted on; but more was missing still. It lay dormant for about five hundred years. From that heavy sleep, it awakened to a dazzling day of freedom, giving light to all the cavernous places where oppression had hidden itself, and it cast it out with all its right, though with less cruelty than it had suffered under its domain.

Thus behaves always the great beginnings of a Republic.

In an enslaved France, the year 1789 was followed by a slumber that ended in 1793 in an explosion which gave its light of freedom to the entire universe, decreeing with a firm hand the destruction of absurd lordships and thrones, not worthy of our times, of feudalism that was depressing and sterilizing, in other words, of slavery, which extinguished and usurped the sovereignty of an always noble and worthy people.

But Spain itself, didn't it sleep for six years under a foreign power which shouted freedom and administered slavery?

All peoples have slept that last sleep of servitude, to awaken invincible and place themselves at the level of the tyrant. Cuba has slept its last sleep. It awakens, it collects its armies and is ready to kill the vile subjugation that dishonors it. Have mercy on anyone who comes in its way!

Cubans! The voice of responsibility speaks to you! Listen to the cries of your homeland!

The despicable regard, enjoyed by those who live in our homeland, is owed to ten years of a war full of episodes that would cover any peoples with glory.

Let us oppose again and for the last time, with the cutting edge of a liberating army, the restrictive policies of our oppressors. We are in our right.

Let us oppose with the decisive will of a people who flourish in the world of freedom, of a people who can no longer be enslaved, the special laws and the repression of a government illegitimate since its inauguration.

There is no argument against our argument.

In Cuba, there is no press, it is a ridiculous simulation; there are no rights of any kind, it's a vulgar joke; taxes are exorbitant, it's a degrading exaction; misery rises and threatens us; that is inconceivable.

We have riches, yes; we have commerce, we have industry, we have education, but all is trampled by the steel foot of a devastating phalanx hungry for gold, even if it is stained by blood, innocent blood. That pillaging plant ruins our soil. The inhuman claws of a selfish government spill blood which waters our soil and sterilizes it, kills our vegetation, destroys our agriculture.

Cubans, no more truces; fellowmen, no more waiting. Cuba calls us to our responsibility, calls us for help, shows us our place.

And our place is in the war of independence.

Death to ultramontanism*!

War on monopoly!

Independence!

Freedom!

This is the call of duty!

These are the cries of the homeland!

Translated by Carolina Hospital.

---

*Historically, of the party of the Roman Catholic Church advocating the doctrine of papal supremacy (*Translator's note*).

CUBA AND THE COLORED RACE

IV

Freedom does not allow for compromise.

One cannot be half free, like one cannot be half enslaved.

Almost all historians, especially the Spaniards, despite their contradictory spirit concerning the virtues of the Negro race, have taken upon themselves to tell the intellectual world that "that" race does not encompass the atrocious collection of abominations that have been heaped upon it. So much wrong can be said about a community, that it can turn into its most favorable panegyric.

The colored race has come to occupy the attention of all the high cabinet posts. Its future has been discussed by all: by some because of their own interest; by others to follow the current trend of the epoch.

And to whom do we owe that the civilized nations have so closely focused their attention on that race, which with more or less prudence all have subjugated?

We owe it to these same detractors. First to the English, from 1727 until 1811, with a cabinet battle for the period of eighty-four years to decide that the Negro should not be enslaved. Eighty-four years of crude debates were needed to define the Negro as a man in erudite England! Finally, the problem was resolved there. The Spanish are left, who after 1814 are resolving the same matter; and although they attentively witnessed the struggles of the English, still today the Spaniards have not come to a resolution.

Would it be too far-fetched to add eighty-four and sixty-seven: 151 years that Spain has been facing the issue, the issue of the abolition of the largest infamy of humanity. One hundred and fifty years to rehearse the drama!

Translated by María Elena Valdés.

From an article also published in *El Separatista*, part of a series of essays titled "Cuba and the Colored Race."

BONIFACIO BYRNE

*B*onifacio Byrne (1861–1936) is considered the number-one exponent of patriotic verse in Cuba. His name is most associated with the poem "My Flag" ("Mi Bandera"), one of the most popular and frequently recited Cuban compositions. Byrne had been living in Tampa during the War of Independence. After the war, he enthusiastically sailed from Tampa for Havana. As he approached the coast of Cuba, he was shocked to see a ship flying both the Cuban and the United States flags. This image inspired him to write the poem "My Flag," which we have included here.

Byrne had been born in Matanzas. By the age of nineteen, he had founded two newspapers and, in 1893, published his first book of poems, *Excéntricas.* He was actively involved in the political turmoils of the island and managed to leave the island in 1895. He settled in Tampa and worked as a reader in a tobacco factory. He continued his activism from Florida, founding the Revolutionary Club of Tampa and writing political commentaries for newspapers such as *Patria, El Porvenir,* and *El Expedicionario.*

Back in Cuba in 1899, he returned to Matanzas and dedicated his life to public service, first as secretary to the provisional government and later as school superintendent. He was a prolific writer and continued his literary endeavors in poetry, as well as experimentations with theater and fiction. He died in Matanzas in 1936.

MY FLAG

*R*eturning from a distant shore,
with my soul in mourning and somber,
I eagerly searched for my flag
and found next to my own another!

Where is my Cuban flag,
the most beautiful flag that exists?
From the steamship I saw it this morning,
and I have not seen a sadder thing! . . .

With the faith of austere souls,
I insist with profound energy
that two flags do not need to fly
where it is enough with one: my own!

In the fields that today are a cemetery
it has seen the brave men fighting,
and has been the honorable shroud
of the poor, dead warriors.

Proudly it hung in the battle
without puerile, romantic display:
Any Cuban who does not trust it
must be whipped for great cowardice!

In the depths of dark prisons
it did not hear the smallest complaint,
and its footprints in other regions
are markers of light in the snow . . .

Do you not see it? My flag is that one
that has never been mercenary
and on which a star shines brighter,
the more solitary it is.

From exile in my soul I brought it
among my dispersed memories
and I have known how to render it homage
by making it fly in my verses.

Although it waves languid and sad
I want the sun
to make it glisten — it alone! —
on the plain, in the sea and on the summit.

Even if some day my flag
is torn bit by bit into pieces . . .
our dead, arms in the air
will know how to defend it still! . . .

Translated by David Miller and Carolina Hospital.

JUANA BORRERO

*J*uana Borrero (1878–1896) was an artist and poet from a distinguished literary family. Her father, Esteban Borrero Echeverría, was a poet, essayist, and political activist; her sister, Dulce María Borrero, was also a poet and a social activist, often writing about educational problems, and the problems of women in society. Her grandfather and uncle, Manuel, were poets as well, and in 1895, a collection of their works (except for Dulce María who was still too young) was published under the title *Grupo de familia*. Juana herself was considered a child prodigy, for, at only twelve years of age, she wrote "Apollo" and "The Daughters of Ran" (both included here), two Modernist sonnets considered among the best in Cuban literature.

She developed as a painter as well as a poet. She began her studies at the prestigious art academy of San Alejandro at ten years of age. She also traveled twice to New York on scholarship to continue her art studies. Her father, Esteban Borrero, took advantage of both occasions to travel with her and engage in revolutionary activities with exiles abroad, such as Martí. Back home, she began a close friendship with the poet Julián del Casal whose work she admired and emulated. Eventually she became engaged to another poet, Carlos Pío Uhrbach. Their marriage was never consummated.

The Borrero family lived in Havana until the start of the War of Independence, when the family was forced to leave the island because of the father's political activism. The family settled in Key West. Upon their arrival, they stayed at the famous Hotel Duval. Soon they moved to a typical wooden Key West house on Duval Street, above a furniture store.

While living in Key West, Borrero would regularly attend meetings at the San Carlos Institute on Duval Street, where her father would occasionally lecture. She continued to write poetry and letters to her fiancé, but seemed detached from the pro-independence fervor that overwhelmed the Cuban community on the key. Her health began to decline. She suffered fevers and overall weaknesses which were not diagnosed for months. Finally, without seeing her fiancé, Carlos Pío, one last time, she died. In 1896, at the young age of eighteen, while still in Key West, Juana Borrero died of typhoid fever, but not before leaving more of her masterful verses, such as "The Last Rhyme" (also included here), which she wrote on her deathbed. She was buried in Key West. Carlos Pío joined the revolutionary forces soon after her death and died a horrible death himself in the jungle. His remains were never found. The Borrero family returned to Cuba in 1899, without Juana.

Almost a hundred years after Juana Borrero's death, Belkis Cuza Malé, another Cuban artist and poet, also in exile in Florida, would write Borrero's story in the biography *El Clavel y la Rosa: Biografía de Juana Borrero*.

APOLLO

*M*ade of marble, brilliant and proud,
sweetness crowns his face,
his hair falling in curls
around his forehead so pure.

Binding my arms to his neck
and constraining his splendid beauty,
with joy and good fortune
my lips eagerly mark his white forehead.

Against his immobile, tightened breast,
I adore his indifferent beauty,
and wanting to revive it desperately,

carried by my delirious lover,
I leave a thousand kisses of burning tenderness
extinguished there upon the cold marble.

Translated by David Miller.

THE DAUGHTERS OF RAN

*E*nveloped among diamond-like foams
that sprinkle their rosy bodies,
the wavelets surge from the sea in a group
illuminated by the rays of the sun.

Covering their migratory backs
the unbraided hairs descend,
and at the murmur of the waves, the echoes
mingle with their silvery smiles.

Thus they live content and happy,
between the sky and the sea,
ignoring perhaps that they are beautiful,

and the waves, themselves among rivals,
collide with one another, crowded with foams,
narrowing their virginal forms.

Translated by David Miller.

LAST RHYME

I have dreamed in my mournful nights,
in my sad nights of sorrows and tears,
with a kiss of impossible love
without thirst nor fire, without fever nor desires.

I do not want the delight that weakens,
the panting delight that burns;
the sensual lips that kiss and stain
cause me infinite boredom.

Oh, my beloved! My impossible beloved!
My lover dreamed from a sweet glance,
when you kiss me with your lips,
kiss me without fire, without fever nor desire.

Give me the kiss dreamed in my nights,
in my sad nights of sorrows and tears,
that it might leave a star on my lips
and a tenuous perfume of spikenard in the sun.

Translated by Carolina Hospital.

JOSE MANUEL CARBONELL

*J*osé Manuel Carbonell (1880–1968) was a poet, politician, diplomat, and scholar. He was born in Alquizar, Havana, but his family emigrated to Florida when he was still a boy. He was raised and educated in Tampa; there, he continued to be dedicated to the land of his birth, as the two poems included here show, both written while still living in Tampa. He also became active in the revolutionary movement and started the magazine *The Expeditionary* (*El Expedicionario*). Eventually, he joined the military forces and embarked on a revolutionary mission to the island, becoming a lieutenant.

After independence, he was very active in Cuban politics and in promoting culture and the arts. In 1902, he founded the Ateneo of Havana. In 1909, he became Superintendent of Schools; he also directed several literary and cultural magazines, and served as president of the National Academy of Arts and Letters for fourteen years. Furthermore, he frequently traveled abroad, representing Cuba at international conferences, in addition to serving as the Cuban ambassador to Mexico.

He is probably best known for his eighteen-volume series on the evolution of Cuban culture from 1608 until 1927 (*La Evolución de la Cultura Cubana*), published in 1928. His own poetry was marked by a strong sense of patriotism and independence. He published several collections of poems, including *Arpas* in 1904 and *La visión del águila* in 1908. He did much to promote the works of other writers as well: he supervised the publication of complete works by Gertrudiz Gómez de Avellaneda, José Jacinto Milanés, Jesús Castellanos, and others.

SONG OF THE FREE

*S*laves, awaken! From your pains,
freedom will liberate your only yearning;
the sad sound of the chains will no longer
extend your barbarous agony.

Slaves, awaken! Hurl to the wind
shouts of rebellion against the tyrant;
display the fateful, bloody saber,
draw the blood through the fertile plain.

Slaves, awaken! Erect your haughty forehead
with noble, arrogant soul,
let the cruel despot be humiliated
seeing the tricolor flag afloat!

Oh, homeland, oh, sweet love of my soul,
oh, unforgettable, enchanted ground,
to see you free and respected one day
I would dare to climb the sky!

And at last you will be free. Upon the earth
that today nurtures the faith of your sacrifice,
the bugles of war will play
the triumphant hymn in strident sound.

Tampa, 1896.

Translated by David Miller and Carolina Hospital.

JOSE MANUEL CARBONELL

BLIND LOVE

*O*h homeland, in the sorrowful
night of existence

you are the miraculous,
luminous rose
that enlightens my conscience.

I do not know why I love you
with blind adoration,
but because of your faith I die;
your life is mine! . . .

Tampa, 1896.

Translated by Carolina Hospital.

AGUSTIN ACOSTA

A̶gustín Acosta (1886–1979) was a poet known for his contribution to the Modernist movement. He published ten books of poetry, including *Ala* in 1915, and was named National Poet in 1955. "The Sugar Harvest" *(La Zafra)*, probably his best-known work, an excerpt of which is included here, is an almost epic poem that explores the Cuban national identity through the process of the sugar harvest. At the same time that the poem praises the beauty of the Cuban landscape, it warns against North American imperialism.

Acosta began his writing at a young age. By the time he was fifteen, some of his verses had been published in *El Jejen*, the paper of his home town, Matanzas; his work later appeared in important Havana magazines. Acosta's poems reflected the influence of his favorite writers, Ruben Darío and Federico Uhrbach, another Cuban Modernist poet who resided in Florida at the turn of the century.

Acosta attended the University of Havana, earning a law degree in 1916. He became a notary public and settled in a small town near Matanzas in the heart of the sugar industry. It was here that he became closely acquainted with the process of sugar making, an inspiration to his famous poem and a catalyst for his political activism.

Because of his protests during the Machado government, he served a prison sentence; however, after the 1933 revolution, he was elected governor of Matanzas and later senator. He was also an academic and translator. After the 1959 revolution, he suffered political imprisonment again because of his opposition to the regime and eventually left the island for the States in 1972. Two years after his arrival in Miami, he published *El apóstol y su isla* (1975), a recompilation of his best poems, and *Trigo de Luna* (1978), his last book, an anthology of love poems noted for its beauty and tenderness. He died in exile in Miami in 1979.

THE SUGAR HARVEST

Canto II

Noon on the Fields

*I*t smells of sugarcane. Upon the green
surf of the canefields
there is a tremor of sun, a rippling,
an impalpable vibration
that toasts the straw sheath
of the erect fruits.

The earth's red clay,
dried up without
the rain, shows the indelible tracks
of cartwheels and oxen hooves,
now pools of blood . . .

The air scorches. Hardly a shade appears
on the ground to
cool the red paths
and ripen into gold, orange groves or
into sweetest purple, star apples,
episcopal
universes of fragmentary pulp.

There is a vague odor of sugarcane in the air,
and the oxen rest on the blond pasture,
with that placidity that withdraws them
from all temptation. Above the oxen,
meditative and polygonal,
blackbirds skip — crow with spirit —
as black as the NO that life
is in the habit of giving hope. The cornfields

79

lose their golden grains beneath the beak
of the happy birds. The air
is a blue crystal that makes visible
all the green shade of the trees;
and above all the immense emerald,
Atlantic of the canefields,
the sun is a crystal that purifies itself,
and the wind is a crystal that goes on a voyage . . . !

The fruit hopes for the cold
to mellow its sweet juice.
But if the stalk in each cane elevates
its grey tuft to the air,
like a long Guinea-hen feather
that resists the sudden gusts of wind,
— year of ruin . . . ! The peasant will predict,
from the shadow of his old tree . . .

Nothing remains for the peasant to do
but wait. He examines the ropes
that help the cart
hoist the cane. The plows
sleep, darkened with mud, in the usual
places. The impatience of chickens
predicts the dawn in the barnyards;
the grindstone reveals its metallic hunger
to the cutlass;
the hanging lantern changes oil;
the yokes and yoke-pads are fixed;
and while the sugar mill nearby,
raising its hard, domineering tower,
makes the strategic order for the attack,
pleasant dreams of a bountiful sugarcane harvest
spread through the farms
and there is a strong odor of sugarcane in the air . . .

Translated by David Miller and Carolina Hospital.

RUBEN MARTINEZ VILLENA

*R*ubén *Martínez Villena* (1899–1934) was known as a poet, fiction writer, and political activist. He was born in Alquizar and grew up in Havana. From a young age, he showed both political and literary inclinations. In high school, he was elected president of the student body, and later he studied at the University of Havana. In 1912, he received a doctorate in public law and in 1913, one in civil law.

While practicing law, Martínez Villena also joined a literary group. During this time, he began to write his best-known avant-garde poems, such as "The Giant," "The Sleepless Pupil," and "Insufficiency," included here, and found in his only collection of poetry, *La Pupila Insomnia (The Sleepless Pupil),* published posthumously in 1936. His short stories and some of his essays were also published in 1940, in the collection *Un Nombre (A Name).*

In 1923, Martínez Villena became the leader of the university student movement and joined the group Veterans and Patriots, with whom he traveled to Key West to practice bombing flight strategies in the hopes of overthrowing the government of de Zayas. Instead, he spent a month in jail in Ocala, Florida, and ended up as a dishwasher in Ybor City at a beer factory before returning to Cuba.

Villena was affiliated with the Communist Party in Cuba and served several prison terms there for his activities. After a twenty-four-hour strike against Gerardo Machado, in May of 1930, Martínez Villena was sentenced to death; however, he exiled himself in the United States. On his way to New York, he spent some days in Florida again, in both Key West and Jacksonville. By then, he had contracted tuberculosis. From New York, he was sent by friends to a sanatorium in the Caucasus in the Soviet Union, but did not find a cure. He died in Cuba in 1934. In his later years, as his political activism increased, he denied all poetry, including his own.

THE SLEEPLESS PUPIL

I have the grim impulse and the sacred yearning
to see in life the sleep of a dead man.
Oh, this sleepless pupil under this closed eyelid!
I shall sleep, soon enough, with an open eyelid!

Translated by Carolina Hospital.

THE INSUFFICIENCY OF THE SCALE AND THE IRIS

*L*ight is music in the throat of the lark,
but your voice must be made from the same darkness:
the wise nightingale alters the shadow
and translates it into the sonorous iris of its dirge.

The visible specter has seven colors,
the natural scale has seven sounds:
you can braid them all in diverse songs,
yet your greatest sorrow will remain unspoken.

Dominating the scale, dominator of the iris,
you will silence the impossible song in darkness.
It has to be black and mute. Your verse must fail

to express the key of your secret anguish,
an inaudible note, of another, higher octave,
a color, from the dark, ultraviolet region.

Translated by David Miller.

THE GIANT

*W*hat am I doing here where there is nothing
great to do? Was I born so alone in order
to await the days,
the months, the years?
To await who knows
what that does not come, that cannot
ever come, that does not even exist?
What is it I wait for? God! What is it I wait for?

There is a concentrated,
sullen, expectant force
in the deepest part
of my being, there is something,
there is something that reclaims
a dark, formidable purpose.

It is the imprecise
yearning of a tree; the impulse
to ascend and ascend until I can
render mountains and amass stars!
Growing, growing as far as the immeasurable!

Not by the smooth
pleasure of the ascension, not by the futile
vanity of being large . . .
but by measuring myself, face to face,
with the Lord of the Black Dominions,
with anyone who disdains
my creeping worm's smallness,
talentless, inept, weak, not created
in order to struggle with him, and who nevertheless,
rejoices in harassing me and all born men
with his questions

and his derision, and spits and surrounds us
with his tightened net of interrogators!

Oh mystery! Mystery! I sense you
as an adversary worthy of the giant
who sleeps a torpid dream beneath the brain:
beneath this immobile brain that protects
and in its concave walls makes obstacles of
the uncertain gestures and the somnambulant,
ingenuous furies of the giant.
Awaken, the sleeping crouched one
who appears to keep an eye on your
steps in the darkness! Hurry!

And no one responds to me, nor is it possible
to shake off the drowsiness of the centuries
increased in modern narcotics
of doubt and ignorance; oh, the useless
effort! And the drowsiness grows and grows
behind this trembling fatigue!

And you pass, perhaps if I hope for it,
the unique one, the great one, who deserves
the captivated offering of the mind
and the poor holocaust of life
for breaking a knot, only an old,
interrogative knot without reply!

And you pass, the eternal, the immutable,
the unique and total, the infinite,
mystery! And I grab
with both tremulous, convulsed hands,
the brain split open, and I ask myself
what am I doing here, where there is nothing, nothing
great to do? And in the darkness no one
hears my desolate cry. And I continue
shaking the giant!

Translated by David Miller.

CARLOS MONTENEGRO

*C*arlos Montenegro (1900–1981) was a novelist, short-story writer, and journalist whose turbulent life served as a source for many of his autobiographical fictions. His life started tranquilly enough in a small town in Galicia, Spain, as the son of a Cuban mother and Spanish father. When Montenegro was seven years old, the family moved to Havana, where they remained until 1914, when they spent nine months in Argentina. Upon his return to Havana, Montenegro served as an apprentice to a shipwright in exchange for room and board. He sailed on long journeys around Central and South America and was occasionally incarcerated for smuggling. In 1919, he mortally wounded one of a group of attackers; in spite of his claims of self-defense, he was sentenced to prison at the fortress El Castillo del Príncipe where he remained from 1919 until 1931.

While in prison, he made use of the library to teach himself and began to write short stories. While still in prison, he received a magazine award for his story *El Renuevo*. Montenegro eventually published three books of short stories, a novel, two plays, and two pamphlets. His novel *Hombres sin mujer* (*Men Without Women*) deals with homosexuality in the prison system. In its content, diction, and fatalistic end, it situates Montenegro in a post-naturalist, modern era with other great short-fiction writers such as Horacio Quiroga.

After his release from prison, Montenegro joined the Communist Party in Cuba and participated in the Civil War in Spain as a correspondent. In 1941, however, he resigned from the party and worked with Rolando Masferrer to expose corruption at the highest levels of the Cuban Communist Party. In 1944, he won the literary prize "Hernández Catá" for a short story and began the magazine *Gente* which he later turned over to his wife Emma Pérez Tellez, a professor of literature. This was a quiet and solitary period for Montenegro.

When Castro took power in 1959, Montenegro exiled himself in Costa Rica until 1962, when he moved to Miami. There he lived humbly, almost anonymously, for almost 20 years, until his death in 1981. While in Miami, he collaborated in the weekly *Libertad*, where he published some of his stories, and wrote his last novel, *El mundo inefable*, based on his prison experience in Mexico in 1917 during the Mexican Revolution. His novel *Hombres sin mujer* was reprinted in 1981, while he was still in exile in Miami.

MEN WITHOUT WOMEN

A Stone in the Way

When he entered the prison, his conscience, that of an uncultured man, was shocked by so much filth. He could not believe what he saw happening right under the vigilance of the prison guards and in spite of so many punishments. His first reaction was disgust, later, indignation, and finally, he became used to it, but avoiding any contact, concealing himself in the corners. . . . Each time he had gotten close to someone, he had discovered, to a greater or lesser degree, that shameful vein; some brought it from the street, from the city; to him they all seemed like lepers who were going to contaminate him. Those he found who thought like him quickly changed their minds, either because it was the general trend or because they thought him exaggerated or too demanding. . . . What else could be possible there? . . . A man deprived of a woman year after year ends up discovering in another man what he misses, what he needs so much that even in dreams his blood boils, and awake, it permeates all his thoughts and turns them into a mortar which invisible fingers sculpture into a thousand different ways, all pointing to the abnormal, to madness. It doesn't matter if suddenly you don't see flesh: sex is in everything. It is hidden, in the sock of Don Juan; in the one who has domesticated a spider; in the one who has embraced *Allan Kardec*. . . . It is solicitous in the madness of Valentín, even at the moment he smacks with his inert arm his deadly blows. . . . It is everywhere: in the corners, behind the columns, everywhere where a bit of shade or sunshine falls; it lies especially on the sheets of the mats, in the rule that prohibits the use of soap or talcum powder. . . . In the climate!

But Pascasio remained unaffected; for him, all of it was disgusting. . . . How was it possible for a man to seduce another man? . . . He had ended up laughing effusively. . . . Come on! He too could do with . . . And had blood . . . And was potent . . . And . . . Blasted! . . . But, when he was desperate, he would dream of Encarnación, of Tomasa, of a broom or whatever, but with skirts, and, done, he

---

Excerpt from *Men Without Women (Hombres Sin Mujer)*, a novel originally published in Cuba and reprinted in Mexico while Montenegro was in exile in Miami.

was ready for the next one! . . . If not, he had his kettles in the kitchen, large and heavy like a man. . . . He moved them from here to there and tired himself out. . . . He knew that a day of intense labor would calm him, and if he didn't bathe later, better yet. Tired and dirty he would throw himself in the corner of the yard and take his nap, not without taking count of how much prison time he had left, subtracting the time he would get off for good behavior. At night, when he was locked up in the cell, he didn't speak to anyone; one hundred men screamed into his silence, but he remained antagonistically silent, day-dreaming, absorbed in thoughts that would transport him far away from his present reality, either to the past or to the future upon his release. . . .

But now, suddenly, everything had become complicated: there was a stone in his way. He had had to strike Candela, and who knows what awaited him concerning the business with La Morita. . . . He knew from experience that to be gossiped about by the prisoners was the same as falling into a river without knowing how to swim. . . . And now he was slipping, with his feet already touching the water, holding on so the current wouldn't drag him in.

First, it was Candela, later Comencubo. Who would be next? He made a fist with one hand and caressed it with the other. . . . But, what about the two months of good conduct he was about to earn? What if he went straight to the prison authorities and reported it all?

He made a gesture of repugnance. He hated stool pigeons more than the effeminates, plus, wasn't it a mockery to stand in front of the prison authorities and admit that another man was wooing him? . . . Perhaps they would decide to have a hearing and he would have to appear in front of all the prisoners with La Morita, Comencubo, and Candela. Only thinking about it made him shudder. The authorities would say: "What is happening prisoner 5062, Pascasio Speek?" La Morita would sneer at him and everyone would laugh. . . . God damn them all!

Pascasio got himself agitated, as if the moment had come, with fists clutched and a defiant look. The men who worked around him looked at him surprised. One of them said:

—What is wrong, buddy? Are you showing off?

And turning to the person next to him, added in a whisper:

—I have yet to see one of these who hangs around alone in the corners end up all right. They all end up, sooner or later, messed up. . . . They always have something going on!

Pascasio wiped his brow with the back of his hand. The fierce expression on his face had been replaced by impotence. He was disoriented. Suddenly he felt his total alienation, his loneliness. . . . He was a man lost in a desert; those surrounding him were hostile, but, barren like the sand. He was too tired to reach his goal. . . . Until that moment he had been able to endure alone, but he understood that he was disarmed, that the entire prison came between him and his liberty; he was defenseless, without a friend in whom to trust, without even a machete in front of an entire sugarcane field to do what Valentín, the crazy one, had done, until he became exhausted, or until he was alone for real, everything at his feet in a million pieces. . . .

On the other hand, here he was discouraged, with the heat of the ovens under his belly like a curse; feeling more distant from the men who surrounded him than from the iron boilers. These, at least, helped him consume his energies in oozings of sweat.

Realizing he had become the center of attention, he made a great effort to explain:

—It's nothing . . . A charcoal chip got in my eye.

And while he forced a smile, he could hear through the noise of the conveyers in the kitchen, the chatter of Valentín, the crazy one:

—I am Don Valentín Pérez Dayson! . . . A black man, a vulture pigeon, a monkey, realize you all that to be white is a career! . . .

Translated by Carolina Hospital.

LYDIA CABRERA

Lydia Cabrera (1899–1992) is one of Cuba's most famous female writers. Her devotion to documenting Cuba's African folklore has made her contributions unique and invaluable to Cuban history and culture. Both *Cuentos negros de Cuba*, a collection of stories that reveal Afro-Cuban legends, myths, and beliefs, and *El monte*, a rigorous study of the African gods and their transformation into Catholic deities, have been translated into numerous languages and have received international acclaim.

Cabrera was born in New York City to a well-known Cuban historian, Raimundo Cabrera. She grew up in Havana and began to write social commentaries at a very young age. In 1922, she left for Paris to study art and remained there for seventeen years. In Paris, she no doubt became aware of the growing European interest in African cultures and revisited her own childhood interests in Afro-Cuban folklore. Back in Cuba, she served as a consultant to the National Institute of Culture. Both as a scholar and as a writer, she contributed greatly to the understanding and interest many hold for Afro-Cuban cultural traditions.

In 1960, after the Cuban Revolution, Cabrera went into exile in Florida. In Miami, she continued to publish more books on Afro-Cuban themes, such as *Ayapá, Cuentos de Jicotea*, in 1971; *Yemayá y Ochún*, in 1974; and *Los animales en el folklore y la magia de Cuba*, in 1988. She also lectured, until she became too frail. The scholar and writer Isabel Castellano, with whom Cabrera lived during the last five years of her life, has been instrumental in promoting the importance of Cabrera's legacy. Lydia Cabrera died in Miami in 1992, after a long life of dedication to her work.

HOW THE MONKEY LOST THE FRUIT
OF HIS LABOR

*J*uan Ganga told his wife, "I think I'll clear an acre and plant some rice."

"Go ahead, do whatever you want," answered Viviana Angola.

Juan Ganga almost never finished what he started. His enthusiasm invariably waned by noontime.

But this time Juan Ganga was determined to harvest rice.

He spent a day leveling the field. He cut down a tree or two. The next morning, finding the entire field cleared, he gathered sticks until vespers. The following day, he found all the deadwood burned. He returned at daybreak with a hoe and hoed leisurely until sunset. When he returned the next dawn, the land was completely hoed.

Ah! The rice had ripened and Juan Ganga happily decided that the moment had arrived to show off his work to Viviana Angola before beginning the harvest. But then a monkey arrived and told him, "Juan Ganga, the rice is ready for reaping. When are you going to begin?"

"I thought I'd start tomorrow."

"Very well, but you won't be alone. We have both worked on this field and I, too, have every right to profit from my work. Isn't that fair?"

"Yes, sir."

"You come tomorrow with your helpers and I'll come with mine. I'll have a hundred monkeys with me. You begin with your folk at one end of the field and I'll start harvesting on the other side with the monkeys until we meet in the middle somewhere. And whoever gathers more, well . . . isn't that fair?"

That afternoon, Juan Ganga returned home discouraged, gloomy. He didn't dare – it pained him – to tell Viviana Angola what had happened, for each time she had heard him boast of how swiftly he had levelled, cleared, hoed, and planted his acre, she had done nothing more than say "Hum!" To have to confess to her . . . still, Viviana Angola could fix anything. What a woman! Whenever her name was mentioned, people always said. "That woman is worth her weight in gold" or "She's priceless." Basking in the envy of others, Juan Ganga himself proudly affirmed, "My woman is worth as much as any man." There was one and only one Viviana Angola in the land. . . . Certainly Viviana scolded him and even punished him, hurling at him the first hard object she could grasp. But it's also true that whenever Viviana got angry, she was always in the right, and her outbursts were only fleeting. Her rages, no matter how justified, never lasted more than a few seconds. Once the dangerous moment of the explosion passed, all her anger vanished. Her happy disposition and jesting nature, coupled with her heart of gold, made her forgive very quickly. Yes. Viviana forgave all, everything. She had as great a capacity for pardon as for work and happiness!

Juan Ganga would have given anything to take her to his field and show her his ripe rice to prove that he hadn't lied, that he had worked. Covering himself with glory in her eyes, he could have told her, "There! You see?"

Now, she didn't know how to explain it, but when Viviana Angola saw him so discouraged and pensive, with such decreed eyes fixed on the ground, she suspected something serious: "Juan Ganga, you tell me what's wrong this very minute."

And Juan Ganga told her everything.

"I'm sunk! Lost! One hundred good men couldn't finish in days what those monkeys could do in only a few hours."

"We'll figure a way out of this scrape," said Viviana Angola. And since she couldn't go long without laughing for one reason or another – no one in this world ever laughed with such pleasure nor had a more contagious laugh – Viviana greeted Juan Ganga's predicament gleefully.

"You don't understand, Viviana. Those monkeys are unstoppable. They pick ten plants where they've only sown five!"

Finally, Viviana Angola, who never walked but ran, hurried away to buy a bunch of jingle bells.

"Jingle bells?"

"Leave it to me. I know what I'm doing."

Then she went to look for the men needed to help harvest the rice. Fifty would be enough if they all worked together; she rounded them up.

Viviana Angola showed up at the rice field at God's sunrise, followed by Juan Ganga and his assistants. The monkeys were already waiting there. They stood in the middle of the field, between the two sections.

The men took one side; the monkeys, the other; Viviana Angola stood in the center. The Chief Monkey gave the signal: "Begin!"

The two groups advance across the field. The men aren't exactly falling asleep, but Juan Ganga is right. As hard as they try, they can't keep up with the monkeys. While the men bundle one sheaf, the monkeys do six.

Juan Ganga crosses his arms.

"We're sunk!"

But Viviana Angola doesn't lose heart. Smiling and vivacious, she begins to gently sway, swinging her shoulders and back as she chants:

> Ayelele ta kunde
> Kuna makando munango
> endile!

Soon there is a rich, enchanting melody that stirs the curiosity of the industrious monkeys.

"Listen," they tell one another, interrupting their work and straining their ears.

Viviana Angola sings. . . .

She turns toward the men and gently lifts the hem of her skirt. Then she turns toward the monkeys and raises her skirt to her waist. Oh!

"Look!" the monkeys shriek, overjoyed.

"Look! Just look!"

Viviana Angola shakes her hips suddenly:

> Goringoro-goro-goro-goro. . .

"And do you hear that? She rings!" they say, more amazed each time.

"Did you see? . . . "

"Yes. . . ."

"Oh!"

"Wait! – look again!"

"Now – look! Now! Now! Listen! And do you *see?*"

Viviana Angola turns toward the part of the field where the men work unceasingly. She shows her ankle. . . .

The monkeys and their Chief stand rooted, absorbed . . . staring.

Then Viviana Angola turns toward them; one moment she shows them – a second, no more – just what keeps ringing and sparkling.

> Goringoro-goro-goro-goro

Their frenzied curiosity mounting, the monkeys dart about frantically, jumping from side to side but not harvesting rice. No. To get a better look at just what Viviana Angola is concealing, they throw themselves stupidly to the ground, straining to see even more.

Some shriek stupidly, others jubilantly, impatiently. . . .

If Viviana Angola would only stay still a moment with her skirt raised! What does Ma' Viviana have that chimes and shines so?

The monkeys' sheaves have all fallen to the ground; the men snatch them up.

> *Ayele' ta' kunde'*
> *Kuna Makando*
> *endile!*

"Look!"

"Now! . . . Now!

> *Goringoro-goro-goro-goro*

"Oh!"

The Chief, stupidly, also stands there, rooted in place, waiting for Viviana Angola to raise her skirt just once more to satisfy their curiosity. The men keep right on working steadily.

> *Goringoro-goro-goro-goro*

And the monkeys ended up without rice . . . and without ever knowing what was hidden, what was so fascinating, what tinkled and twinkled under the skirts of Viviana Angola.

Translated by Mary Caldwell and Suzanne Jill Levine.

ANIMALS IN CUBAN FOLKLORE & MAGIC

Preamble

Folklore in Cuba is surprisingly rich, due to the importation of Africans to the island almost since the discovery. Mixed at times with Spanish folklore, which the whites have not preserved, in it, the African scholars will find the same topics found in the different ethnic groups taken to Cuba who left their religious beliefs, music, and languages.

Their legends and stories, transmitted orally from generation to generation, never tempted any Cuban student or writer. Perhaps the idea of collecting them, and much less publishing them, would have seemed grotesque or denigrating.

For us, after many years of absence, Cuba seemed to be an inedited country for its children. If its history had not been fully studied, how could we hope that attention be given to its folklore — in spite of the efforts by Fernando Ortiz — and much less to the profound mark left by the African culture, whether we like it or not.

Even knowing no one will waste his time, and much less here in exile, in a country where time is only money, in reading these notes without any practical use, I offer them because there are some countrymen — and those few are enough — to whom distance has allowed them to see, as happened to me in another enchanting and voluntary exile, what they did not see nor feel when near: the unique enchantment of our Island lost — I am afraid — forever.

For these individuals, I offer these stories, that I have gathered by returning to the poetic and marvelous interior world of my childhood, where the same language was spoken by all men, animals, and things.

Excerpts from *Animals in Cuban Folklore & Magic (Los Animales en el Folklore y La Magia de Cuba),* published by Ediciones Universal in 1988 while Cabrera was in exile in Miami.

The Lizard

It attracts good influences in the houses.

A lizard is not susceptible to burning in a fire: in a fire in a sugarcane field all the animals burn. The lizard and the green chameleon turn yellow, but nothing happens to them. The fire doesn't burn them.

The shamans use them for spells; magically, with the tongue of these animals, they attach to a person a bolt of white cloth, half a bottle of spirits, two roots of basil, and the name of the victim of the spell.

— To cause harm you place the green lizard tied up over a pile of filings on which you have poured milk and you leave it a while in order for it to curse the person who has trapped it. The filings moistened by the milk also curse the person, so that both the lizard and the magnet hate it.

Then the shaman loosens it and orders it:

—Bring the wrath of God and take it to So and So.

The lizard rushes to take the evil to the desired victim.

— Men at the beginning of the Earth were lizards. Their hands have fingers like ours. Their skin is like that of snakes, a far relative.

They are messengers of the Orichas.

The souls of the dead penetrate them. It is said they love men and hate women, as is the case with the water snakes.

They are born, like other animals, when Changó thunders.

They are very sensitive to music. Harmless, they appreciate being treated well, and they allow themselves to be domesticated, such as the ones that lived in the garden in the Quinta San José.

But if a cruel knife tears off its tail, as was common in Cuba, the tail contorts a long time and curses the savage who deserves it.

Translated by Carolina Hospital.

ENRIQUE LABRADOR RUIZ

*E*nrique Labrador Ruiz (1902–1991) was a novelist, short-story writer, essayist, and journalist. His fiction works, such as *Carne de quimera,* from which "The Little Rabbit Ulán" included here is excerpted, led the way for the stylistic experimentation that revitalized Cuban fiction. This particular story is considered one of the best in its genre of the fantastic and won the Hernández Catá International Award the year it was published in 1946. *Carne de quimera* was reprinted in 1983 while the author was in exile in Miami. Labrador Ruiz's revolutionary use of magic realism, not yet fully recognized, precedes that of the Colombian novelist García Marquez. Other innovative fiction works include *El Laberinto de si mismo, La sangre hambrienta,* and *Trailer de sueños.* He also wrote several collections of essays and poetry.

The author was born in Sagua la Grande. At the age of five, he moved to Cruces, where he stayed until 1921, when he moved to Cienfuegos to work as a journalist. Only two years later, he moved to Havana and quickly acquired a literary reputation. In 1950, he was awarded the Cuban National Prize in Literature. After Castro took power in 1959, he became disillusioned with the regime and became *persona non grata* until he left the island in 1972. After living in Spain and Venezuela, he settled in Miami where he lived with his wife Che-Ché until his death in 1991.

Cuban novelist Guillermo Cabrera Infante, who has resided in London since the 1960s, has stated that Labrador Ruiz "was one of the great writers of America. He was one of the first, if not the only one with Lino Novas Calvo and Virgilio Piñera, to destroy realism, which in Cuba had acquired a reactionary regionalism."

THE LITTLE RABBIT ULAN

$\mathcal{M}$aité was forty-and-some years of age, was never married, never knew a man. Alone in the world with nothing but the patch of land her father, Don Porfirio Zuaque, left her — he who on the sharp blade of his machete had made it to lieutenant in '95 — she, now and then, paced before her front fence conjuring up the old veteran.

How well she saw him; how well. . . . Once his poor wife was dead, with his pay and some savings, her father had shut himself up in his small patch of land near Havana, a very pretty one with its beds of cassava, some rows of corn, and a vegetable garden that was a delight. Not much, but what more did he want for just the two of them?

Scarred by smallpox, her father's face was imposing. From his lips hung an old pipe gnawed in several places, worn away here and there, with one end plain broken, holding on to it until he swapped it for some cheap cigars from the run-down store in town. Being the apprehensive type, he had become terrified at smoking the pipe once he found out that a neighbor and good friend from *Guatao* had died of mouth cancer, as they said, from always having his pipe hanging religiously from the side of his mouth.

Her father always showed bad faith toward his neighbors, especially to those of his generation who had not participated in the war like he had. He contemptuously referred to them as "pacifists," when he wasn't ranting about "guerrilla fighters" and other abominations which would occur to him.

Impassive, Maité did not try to silence him; it would have come to naught. With all her dignity she picked her flowers, thinking that her father was perhaps a bit demanding, since not all men have the same temper, nor are they all made to the same measure. With her benevolent eyes she would gaze upon her neighbors and it was that delicacy of her personality that spared the old man from more than one hefty quarrel started by his irrepressible foul mouth.

On his deathbed the old man had said to Maité:

"My daughter, never marry a 'pacifist'; you already know how I feel about them. But if you don't find a veteran, a real veteran, let him at least be a man. Not even dead do I want in my family any weaklings or grovelers. . . . Confounded! Brave calamity!"

For having listened so well and followed his advice, Maité stayed single. She was forty-and-some years of age, worked in the vegetable garden, tilled the soil, drew the water, and toiled ceaselessly to improve her fledgling animals and care for her other beasts. Time for anything else she never had. Only that in the afternoons, sometimes, she would call out to the old man, there near the front fence gazing attentively at the setting sun, just in case he might deign to take a peek at how she was behaving.

That she behaved very well, . . . that went without saying. Very well indeed! For no one will deny that her rejection of that neighbor from "La Rosita," Don Sabino Cruz, an old geezer from the ranks of the rural politicians and an eternal pretender to the fine white hands of any woman . . . had something in it that was first-rate; and the door she slammed on Estrada's nose, he who was a high school graduate and could not even read cursive writing; and her sincere rejection of lanky Trino who with others had been quite seductive; all of these were no meager proof. Trino showered her with flowers, composed musical country poetry for her, he had a taste for literature and rustic country girls, and with his head swimming in alcohol had once dared to say: "I'm a gonna marry Maité." But Trino was not someone whose father would have allowed such a thing; for one reason or another, Trino ran around with women and ran away from work; as for his delusions of being an ace, you did not have to be too sharp to see the truth. How many vanished memories!

The years went by, and Maité realized how her beautiful head of hair was thinning. That lustrous mass of thick hair had lost its shine; its metallic blue had turned grayish and sad. And Maité would say to herself: "It don't look like I'm gonna get married after all." It was a shame and a waste. Yet her good heart made up for it with the little animals she kept, which is, as they say, like taking a shortcut to the good side. What devotion she showed those animals! There was never a bird with a broken wing, a dog with distemper, a horse with glanders, nor a cow with carbuncles or *mazamorra* that she did not energetically take care of. She felt infinitely sorry for chirpers and sucklings, and there were times when the castor oil, the *yagruma* leaves, the peppercress roots, and other home remedies went as much back and forth between her house and the barn as does a calabash cup of coffee at a country wake.

In a cinch she would clean harness sores, sew up wounds, apply bandages; she measured her will by her good desire to succeed. Inimical to leisure, she was never scared off by heavy work of any kind, and after her daily chores, she often found time to graft, replant, and even tame the shoots of the wild vines. Her honor and good reputation were beyond reproach. But, Oh God, how she began to tell herself that her virginal body was withering like a foul root; that her hands were turning scaly, and the rectangular piece of skin that was her cleavage was turning an ominous color. Other such thoughts would come to her with their aura of haziness, especially when powdering herself after bathing at the wash-basin, and she began to feel her good cheer drying up. "Maité," she would say to herself, "you're gonna remain a spinster. You're gonna stay no matter what. You're ready."

And she would cry; pacing and more pacing within the four walls of her room made her head spin. In order to banish the terrible omen she would say to herself over again: "I'll do some ironin'; I'm behind on my work." In that place of hers there was nothing left undone, except of course. . . . She looked through the window, her green eyes half squinting: "The corn," she said, "is already ripenin'. How beautiful's the corn when it looks like that. . . ."

She was not getting old, it was that she had aged. Fanning the coals for the iron, she felt like giving away some toys to who knew what children. Something unforseen was making her tender and maternal. "Since my childhood," she thought, "I've buried myself here; I've scared off everyone with my personality; now they don't even bother to look at me; and for what, with this reputation of mine! Oh Papa, and these eyes of mine that are flickerin' out by the moment."

At times she would feel herself born again as if with a live rush, her veins felt on fire, her upper lip would sprout with sweat and beholding herself in the mirror she would make pitiful allowances to herself: "If only one with any shame would come. If only a man, a real man. . . ."

Searching for butterflies for her flower vases she was strutting around the little garden, picking buds because she was in a hurry and she wanted to have more flowers, when she heard a man who with his bandore sang out:

> Be of happy heart, my sweet,
> though late in the day it be:
> for through a heart unhappy
> flows blood of poorest pedigree.

And she felt wounded; wounded right in the chest.

She went into the house shaking. She was frightened by the tone, the music, the intentional lyrics. Her foot on the smoothing iron she told herself: "It serves me right, huh? that goad sent straight at me. . . ." And she went out the back door and set herself to scaring off the blackbird because, even if it ate the ticks on the oxen, ticks are not, after all, enough of a bother to make a fuss over them, and in any case. . . . What is certain is that it disgusted her and she did not want to behold the spectacle.

"Go away, ugly blackbird, go away! Eatin' live bugs. . . ."

But what did any of this have to do with that tight lump she felt at times in her chest? It was a dumb knot which at times disappeared, but which sometimes settled right there in the middle, with unexpected fury, and left her breathless, without so much as letting her gasp. Is it the years? Is it really, really the years? Or is it a fever, some evil fever perhaps? . . .

These ambiguities brought her to think that if she had only found herself a man, then now, . . . now things would not be this way. For a man, if he is good and wholesome as he should be, always does well and heals and sets right the maladies of body and soul and the troubles of the earth and even of heaven. "Truly," she decided, "there is no better truth."

Blaming her melancholy for all the heated imaginings that prospered in her head was her way of pushing back the assumption that her soul was quite separated from her body, something that seemed an undeniable fact. What a shame! But who was going to know that she also waited for a sparkling needle to someday sew the obvious tear.

II

"I'm a losin' my hands," she laughed. "I'm so happy I can barely feel 'em! So happy . . ."

She could not get over her astonishment and was quite careful to feign it. Oh! Ulán, with his blond downy mustache, began to visit the house. On good days he would come by the small patch of land and, in between cries of "hey ho . . . hey ho!" he would attend to the chores and one could imagine him toiling with the oxen. He would rest on top of the usual hill during the cool part of the day.

Apparently he was twenty years old; he was strong, agile, slippery, with maybe a bit of a sneaky look about him. What could it be? Distrust? Jealousy? From whom? What is certain is that at times the memory of the old veteran returned furiously: "Not even dead do I want in my family any pacifists, or . . . " Maité trembled and she told herself: "I'll have many flowers for his anniversary this year; he won't regret it."

Ulán loved black beans and rice as much as his hefty pots of cornmeal gruel, and if he was interrupted while in the middle of the business of eating he would

let out atrocious shrieks. Maité was never able to make him understand the use of
eating utensils; with strong fistfuls he would empty his plate, laugh, then wipe
his hands on his hairy thighs. Then he would romanticize about any old distant
dream, waste hours grooming his fingernails, twisting his little moustache hairs,
and like an angry and treacherous tyrant he would demand obedience to his
every whim.

"I want, I want, I want," that was his eternal nagging, his constant saying.
Oh! How she imperiously called upon herself from the very bottom of her being,
there, where the layers of immemorial slime are so dark and dense. "I want, I
want, I want."

And when she least expected it, she went to bed with him; she could not
avoid it! Afterwards, a fortnight past, something happened, and in little time her
loneliness was peopled by what she thought were children. Day and night she
walked about with these thoughts, and from the bottom of this pit she extracted
only this thought: "I must, in any case, buy some eyeglasses, . . . but these children are as kids always have been, and as for everythin' else they are the envy of
the world." Yet . . .

With a doubtful air it was frequently said that her rare nuptials involved
something more than just a simple union: this father maintained, for everyone
to see, a vivacious reproductive eloquence and an absolute indifference with
regard to the number of his offspring. Hadn't she complained about it in sudden
fright, given the abnormality of the situation, and he, turning his face on the pillow, with ecstatic panic had mimicked the quintessential form of swooning? If he
said anything at all, its burning meaning, it must be confessed, must have been
what made him lose his judgment completely without anything being remedied.

These violent occurrences and other constant mistakes, like turning the
bedroom into a grim seraglio or some strange and scandalous temple, began to
close in on her. She began to ask herself, without really realizing the full extent
of what she asked: "How long is this gonna go on?" And the cunning with which
she armed herself in order to keep up her wavering luck, moving about in the
midst of her bedroom trinkets, would grow sharper as she asked herself: "What
dress shall I wear today? Would he like me to wear makeup? And wouldn't a little soft perfume please him?"

She became worried about one thing. Ulán would not for anything in the
world eat a piece of pork, nor possum, nor venison. Really, poor Ulán was impossible. . . . He hated beef jerky, salad, chicken, beef. And even though his pretty
garden was formerly very fruitful (and with it gave enough for the best of tables),

presently turnips and beets mysteriously were found all chewed up. Also, along the seams of raised earth sometimes would be found all curled up a guilty-looking fine little blond hair.

Who was rummaging around out there at night? She examined the possibilities: it was hopeless; she couldn't figure it out. This new anomaly made her set jealous traps, keep eager watches, or even put the rifle to her shoulder.

Ulán would go to bed whenever he felt like it, with all his rights as a husband since he was the husband. A foul wind that had blown by that place recently brought with it the shadow of the old veteran, who from the top of the stone wall would begin to curse with virulence that which he always cursed and which, not even dead, he had wanted for his daughter. . . .

"Away with you!" Maité would utter, as much upon seeing the owls emerging from their nests as from something secret which made her shiver. "I'm gonna light a candle to that lonely old soul, so that it'll rest."

One day armed men showed up asking:

"Ain't there 'round here someone called Ulán . . . or Julián?"

Maité trembled.

"Ulán Cabezas," said the corporal. "The one that collects eggs . . . that barters money for eggs. Short fella, with a split lip . . ."

Ulán had positioned himself behind the jute sacks. She, exasperated, felt uncomfortable:

"You'd just betta look somewheres else; those gossipers, the one-eared fella and his buddy, they probably know. And if they don't, they'll probably make somethin' up. They's over yonder, lizard watchin', chewin' the fat and gossipin'."

"Well . . . ," they said, "We'll just see about that. Let's see if we can catch 'em, alright?"

Maité felt better.

"That's fine by me. And so, later, alright?"

The corporal said:

"Wouldn't you happen to have some coffee brewin' around?"

And the other one said sarcastically:

"You ain't even offered."

Impossible. What if they came in and started looking around; what if they suspect. If they knew something, she thought quickly, they could say let's see if the jute sacks are hiding something.

"I ain't got no coffee," she said. "I ain't gone to the store in a spell. Next time who knows."

"You sure you ain't got any, Ma'm?"

She gave them such a look that, raising their rifles, taking their hats off again, and curtseying "see ya later, Ma'm," they started down the road with their usual discretion, as well as this absolute certainty: "She's nuts."

She, on the other hand, did nothing more than tell herself: "Lies, lies! This is a plot by the Rural Police. A guy called Ulán Cabezas, who barters eggs for money, who's got a split lip. Ulán! Ulán! And they wanna catch him, sons of bitches. This is a plot . . . "

She continued ruminating like this until the two were out of sight. Later she started to ponder: "But why? Had Ulán done something bad? Was it certain that they were looking for this Ulán? What was it? A crime? Could it be he had stolen something from someone? Or could it be it was some neighbor accusing him, pure gossip . . . about what was going on?"

What was definitely going on was that the house was suddenly crowded with more sounds and cries from babies. In a short time, in less than a mosquito's buzz, in less than what a cock crows . . . well, how should I say? there arrived five boys who, Maité thought, would be good for some efficient help right soon. Strong, energetic, they grew up lawlessly and had it not been for that harelip that they all boasted, they would have been said to be perfect. Pedro, Pablo, Chucho, Jacinto, and José. . . .

With implacable irony, the wind echoed these names, and some of the area's musicians, having to repeat them so many times, even refused to polish them with their music. Pedro, Pablo, Chucho, Jacinto, and José. . . . They were five pups, playful and mischievous: it was a pleasure to see how they climbed everywhere, how they clamored and made a ruckus, and how from one day to the next, they grew taller and became more physically imposing. They were five suns who in Maité's gloomy firmament shone with unexpected splendor.

One day they proposed going swimming at the river gully. Maité jumped: "To the gully, no. That's where the Bogeyman is. The Bogeyman! Can ya'll imagine . . . ?" No swimming.

Their father alleged that real men had nothing to fear from anything; that they should be hard as a rock, although personally speaking, he . . .

Maité's look translated: "Who asked you to butt in? Who said that you have anything to say? Do me a favor and . . . ?" He became silent, played with his moustache, and admired his fingernails.

It must be said that Ulán had been falling back, back, while the others advanced. These kids now dominated the home, the life of the home, everything about the home. Maité, putting one plus one together, later asked Ulán:

"Personally speakin' . . . what d'ya mean by that, Ulán?"

"Well nothin' . . . Psht, nothin'!"

And he shrugged his shoulders.

Personally speaking, what he would have wanted to say (and he was very happy that he hadn't said it) was that the only thing that makes him uneasy is to feel like a leashed dog; the only thing. Not even guards and their rifles; not even the burly sentinels of the cavalry station, nor stories of human snares told by the country folk. But one thing indeed, a leashed dog . . .

She understood him in a heartbeat; she saw his goosebumps; she guessed his trembling, his head turned down. Weighing the effect she said:

"Don't get desperate over such a trifle; don't anguish yourself, Ulán."

And after an intentional pause, with cruel enjoyment:

"Or is it, ya loaf, that ya feel like goin' huntin'?"

How imprudent! Such words made him livid, but it was already too late. Maité noticed it and it made her blush. What in the world got into her! Never before would it have occurred to her to allude to this particular trait in his character. Why had it suddenly come into her mind, like that . . . in an instant? Feminine instinct. For even when to him there was no past whatsoever, and his life began every day quite normally with her kisses over the top of the stone wall, did she not expect to see in his eyes something infinitely timid, atrociously anxious and madly rushing out? Didn't she know?

III

Such had it been for them. . . . Compressed as the first half of her existence had been, to then become ruined by that oppressive condition, one wretched day, while observing behind the tarlatan curtain by her bedroom window, Maité was able to see something jumping irregularly on the grassy floor outside, next to the stone wall. It was something like a sponge, gray, electric, grotesquely shaped. And she went to see what it was.

On the way over she told herself, upon realizing that it had neither feet nor ears: "But how is it possible that this poor creature made it over here? Some gumption!" When she held it in her hands she caressed it and said: "It isn't ugly. And it looks like that other critter. Where is he?" Frightened, the poor little animal looked at her with tender eyes. She caressed it again; she kissed him vigorously; she ran her hand over its blond rump with infinite tenderness. "A rabbit. . .

. . But never before has a rabbit been seen by these parts. . . . I wonder who sent him to me?"

And kissing him with renewed fervor, in a half whisper:

"Sssst . . . I'm going to name him. . . ."

She was thinking of someone, that was certain. All one had to do was look at her. And she then said without hesitation, but also listlessly: "Sssst . . . Listen! Pretty little rabbit . . . There it is: that will be your name, and don't answer back."

Immediately she bundled him up in a striped kerchief she wore over her head and she thought that when next she went to Guatao. . . . "Iodine!" She would always do her medicine shopping personally and "Iodine" was about all she bought. (Meanwhile her dog Bite-n-Run's upper lip trembled. He would have loved to break the rabbit's neck, that cunning intruder. . . .)

A poor neighbor of hers who suffered from güito, very old and very sick, came out to where she was. She was always looking for her to ask her for home remedies to treat her illness, since Maité was very knowledgeable in these things.

"Maité, what you had promised me . . . for my illness."

She didn't even respond; she didn't even look at her, risking the shame of turning her back on one of her neighborhood's sick.

"Ulán Little Rabbit . . . My little rabbit!" And she started running for home without looking anywhere.

The one-eared one and his buddy, on their way, in front of the picket fence, saw the whole scene, eyes blinking; later they heard how the old neighbor buzzed with sarcasm: "Neighbor, for God's sake, it ain't no big deal . . . ," and they spoke to each other, not very loudly, but loud enough so that Maité could discern it:

"How she loves to raise them critters!"

And the other, stuttering with his usual malice:

"Look like she don't like nothin' bu' critters . . ."

Maité yelled at them from afar:

"Git you sloths, you backbitin' gossipers, go to hell."

They then yelled back:

"Spinster!"

"You mower!"

In the middle of all the commotion the rabbit looked at her with tender eyes, with that certain way of his. . . . She might have been born to sustain blows in life, but to get kicked around like that, how could she take it? It could be said that her heart suddenly filled with joy. She went to the corral to get some milk and in an absurd little ritual she blessed her soul's good north.

The poor little animal had a broken foot. She tinkered around with her potions, applied a light coat of iodine so as to not sting the animal, and covered the foot with a bandage of clean rags. It must be noted, if only because it exceeded the normal measure, just how many signs of affection she performed on the rabbit and with what singular attention she continued to encourage and attend to him. She tried her best to see him cross over the threshold into good health, and were it not that it's profane, it could be said that she treated him like christened folk. "What would you like, my little rabbit Ulán? What do you want, my love? What do you want, my darling?": Her eyes dancing and her waist not yet grown, her soul full of a strange sweetness, full of ecstasy, she would smother him with kisses.

No sooner had he started to heal, she made him stay quietly on her lap for long hours, and if he jumped, Maité would instantly undo herself with cautions and tender exhortations: "My love, snuggle up to my flesh; don't jump away from me. My love of loves, do you love me?"

What was certain was that this excessive care did not allow her time for anything else. It was indeed a sort of sweet fatigue that overtook her; a happy double sorrow. She spent long hours with half-closed eyelids, and, under the excuse that the bright sunlight would hurt her eyes, she endured thirst just to not have to go out to the backyard except for the most final of necessities. In the midst of her home's sleepy ambiance she began to see glowing objects, visions, dancing portable things.

Her chores? Her arms crossed, the hours vanished away as she remained attentive only to one strong voice which beat upon her inner conscience with the wings of angels. Her slackness grew, and even when she did not want to give in to the laziness, who will waste time in pushing themselves to do something which they don't need? Lucky that nothing went lacking, and some things just got a bit tight, though it was all the same to her; she no longer even cared to set a good table, but rather who to feed good chunks of raw vegetables.

She wanted to have time to dream about something unforeseen, surprising, and everything else she would get through quickly, immediately thereupon racing to kiss the disquieting sickling: "Ulán Little Rabbit, you are my lord. Who loves Ulán Little Rabbit very much? Why don't you say? . . . "

Following these emotional outbursts, after the cloth that someone destined for her was well warped, one night she dreamt that she had traveled by bus to Oriente Province; a dirty wagon full of men sitting on wooden crates set in the narrow throughway, and next to her a young black boy, a student, who in his hands played around with a bone which he called "sphenoid." This very circumspect, bespectacled young man frequently would say: "How far is Santiago! When will I get to Santiago?" His Christmas vacations didn't even make him smile because the sphenoid had prophesied a fortnight of worry and caution. Then the relic saw that some uncertain person had brought her there from somewhere it did not know; the relic was bought, according to her father, in some horrid place. The lady who is lodged there now reaches out to her, helps her up a flight of very steep stairs. The lady, and this is something that shouldn't end even if in a dream, then offers her white camellias, whimsical magnolias, and even some dahlias like none that she had ever before seen. Then green turtles came to eat the signs they wore on their corollas; later the sphenoid turned into a piano and great accords signed by Dahl, Camelia, and Magnol who, more with their names than with their gyrations, shook the miserable lice on the window.

Why, she asked herself while breathless in the middle of her dream, hadn't she been named Magnolia, Camellia, or Dahlia? This "Maité" . . .

At dawn the rain burst from the sky, a dense rain which lasted three days, electrifying the atmosphere and causing thunder. Wanting to usher the rain along with it, the wind in the giant reed field swept away the thunderous clap of a thousand demons as if it wanted to wail everything down its gullet ten leagues around. Electrified blue tornadoes awoke her shivering with cold. "When water is blessed it must have something," she thought she heard. "It must have something," she repeated. "Something, something . . ."

Yet, can it be known . . . oh! who it was that bellowed out that cry of anguish that bore straight through her entrails? The creeping vine, turned wild, stuck its frayed branches through the gaps in the hollow wall. She thought about cutting it the next day; she thought about fixing up her garden; she thought about taking care of her things. Only that the moan was heard again and this time she only had one idea.

She went to the room where the little rabbit lay on a bed of straw; she froze: he was not there. She looked in the corners, under the ears of corn, among the ripening squashes, the palm fronds on which he might be sleeping, in the hole in the cement wall: he was not there. When she returned to her bed, her soul crushed, half dead from desperation, he, like a child, with the true mannerisms of a child, begged to be taken out of his enclosure; that if there was any shame at all it was in being locked up; that it was better to die than to continue like that; that deep down, oh! he too had feelings. . . . Or had she not noticed?

This monstrous panorama of terrorizing contours was to her, it must be said, rather agreeable. And even though her blood turned to quicksilver, she took steps backward, almost like someone who measures the void which he is about to save in one leap.

"Don't be mean. . . . Take me out of this." And he said finally: "Go already!"

Maité pinched herself. What dream was this? What informed deformity? What tremendous nail was it that was scratching her conscience? What powerful concentration would be necessary to mitigate, without being foolish, this disgrace? She decided. There was no room for doubt; bad boy . . . , poor thing!

Yet this bad boy who asked to be taken out of that savage state suddenly turned into a man. He grew and grew until there appeared blond whiskers, and on his face a look of a perverted young man. Maité heard this arrogant plea:

"Gimme your breasts, do you hear me? I wanna be the one to drink from your breasts, Maité, the taste of life. Come on already!"

He so forced upon her this desire that she, casting aside the menacing vision of her father, with confident determination ripped her dress from her body.

She was left naked. She had to tie down the dog.

A wild rustic music permeated this scene of light and sweet odors, and shrunk for ever the space that mediated between them. After the brief struggle, she thought she heard him say:

"What we need, Maité, is to never separate from each other. Would you like that?"

He said it with a tone halfway between sanctimonious and impudent. She reflected: "Is this desire legitimate? Is it Christian?" And it looks like they answered her: "Take it! It is your good wish, Maité."

From her secret wound there poured forth happiness.

IV

Everything, no matter how late it happens, is known. "I'm a losin' my hands," she laughed. "I can barely feel 'em. I'm so happy!" She couldn't get over her surprise, yet she would feign it.

This fantastical existence came to an end one early morning when several shots along with leashed chase dogs were heard down the narrow path at the back of the house. Maité was frightened and went out to see. "Who goes there? Who goes there? . . ." Nothing! But the commotion was evident.

Ulán, hearing the barking dogs, suddenly began to diminish, became inexpressibly frightened, huddled up even more on the chair where he was now put to sleep, and began to tremble. The stigma were about to appear.

"Ulán, what's the matter? Tell me. . . . It ain't what you think what's scaring you. Calm down, Ulán. I never meant to hurt you when I talked about those things, I swear! Forgive me. . . . And when I go to Guatao . . ."

He continued to diminish, trembling, speechless, looking toward the corral, anxious and beaten.

Perturbed, lost, Maité uttered:

"Forgive me for that, Ulán. Forgive me fo' it all, Ulán Little Rabbit, my little rabbit o' my heart. Forgive me fo' it . . ."

And as if the most gaping underground of the world were pulling her inexorably toward its deepest bosom, at that point the tenacious fallacy unravelled itself and moving its pointy ears it threw itself down suddenly, sniffing the ground, prodigy turned to dust, knot finally untied.

Velvety, with his brilliant eyes like two beads, he did not respond at all to Maité's calls. With elastic movements and a certain characteristic puffing, although it was one of those things about him no one never remembered, he made for the door, drank in the vast aroma of the countryside outside and, abandoning all aspects of his human form, he slithered out through the gaps in the wall. A certain vapor followed him, throwing out sparks, burning, and left a furrow which led all the way to the gully, and beyond it gyrated in the air again and again, fanning Maité's amazement.

Astonished, sighing, Maité broke into an uncontrolled laughter; then she cried and scratched herself. Lying on the floor, suddenly it seemed to her that she was covered by lots of rubble; that it was all burying her under infinite pyramids of candy; that by way of atonement a sulfurous rain scrubbed her from head to toe.

Who would come to rescue her from this complete darkness, from this mental penury of hers? A single cry rises in her heart: Where did he go? There is no room in her heart for this bubbling.

Nevertheless, she made another attempt. She regretted not yet having her eyeglasses; she rubbed her eyes. What agony, like a one-eyed, one-armed, lame stutterer! She rubbed her poor irritated eyes even harder. What anguish, like a deaf, paralyzed, barren woman! Her eyes were emptying out upon her hands.

Who would have dared to say that she had discerned, in that one lucid moment, from the very primeval forest of her instinct, and over all the reduced possibilities, that he now ran, humbly and gloriously, in search of his destiny, to live forever among his own kind without any need of fakery, all after having consummated a happiness of which he never knew a thing?

But one felt like thinking about it. . . . One felt like it.

And the house returned to its complete solitude, emptied of all the aliens of her fantasy, like when her father died, except that now it was sadder and uglier. What a river of tears! The creeping vine became a prison.

Maité went out to the backyard to look at the world that was left her, the abstract world of trees and stones. With a furious gesture she approached the well; she felt for the rim, threw herself upon the curbstone.

She understood that the whole thing had turned back into the real world. The horse, the cow, where had they gone? They must be around there some-where, there. . . . And she began to shoo away the blackbird, for even if it did eat the ticks. . . . The dog followed her.

With her forty-something years, with her horrible widowhood, what was she going to do? She told herself that even if there weren't any blackbirds. . . . The fledgling animals, where were they? They must be around there somewhere, there. . . . As to the crops, forget it. Wouldn't the Old Man knock loudly where she was, wherever she was? Wouldn't he come to defend her?

She came back into the house. In every corner were papers, empty cans, dead leaves, garbage. "One of these days," she thought, "I'm gonna set myself to cleaning up all this. I don't like it when it's like this. . . ." She opened one of the bedroom doors and closed it back up immediately, sighing: "I don't even have a picture. . . ." Dispossessed, but not asleep, her imagination began to comply with the fatal terms of her orbit.

She opened another door like someone knocking off fruit from a tree; the wood let out a creak. "Even it complains," she mused. "We all complain and no one helps us."

In front of the stone wall the one-eared fellow and his buddy were chatting away. The dog howled at them. To which one of them responded:

"Git out ya dog! What d'you lose around here?"

And the other one brandishing a stick in his hand:

"Your mistress? Just get a little lazy and you'll see!"

She could not hear. All she wanted to do was to scare away the blackbird and, if it could only happen, to sleep for a long, long time. . . . (Sleep is not the word.)

Some days later they came by searching for some rosebuds for the town fes-tivals. The one-eared one got to the gist of things immediately:

"And I wonder how that crazy woman's doin'? Jist look at that: the whole damn place's turned into a downright jungle. They told me in Guatao . . ."

"No better and no worse," his companion answered.

"Jist the same, always the same. . .! But . . . m-m-m-m . . . Jist smell that."
He lifted his nose up in the air.

"Holy shit . . . ! Some God-damned bad shit it smells like; smells like a dead
animal."

"It damn sure does. And seein' as to how Maité sure was one to git all
overblown about everythin', ain't it that she's kicked the bucket, the stubborn
bitch . . . , and there she is, splattered, rottin' away all by her lonesome?"

Translated by Ramón Bayardo Rancaño.

EUGENIO FLORIT

*E*ugenio *Florit* (1903–1994) can be considered the most significant Cuban poet of the first half of the twentieth century. His development as a poet responded to contemporary styles and movements in Latin America and Europe. In particular, he is associated with the styles of "pure poetry" and, later, testimonial verse. In Cuba, Florit became involved with the literary group *Avance*, which, in the early decades of the twentieth century, was on the leading edge of avant-garde literary movements. The *Avance* group published Florit's first book, *Trópico*, in 1930.

His personal life can be divided into three stages associated with his residency in Spain, Cuba, and the United States. Florit was born in Madrid to a Spanish father and a Cuban mother. The family returned to Havana in 1918, when he was fifteen years old. He established his reputation there as an important Cuban poet. In 1940, he traveled to New York as a Cuban consul. Five years later, he left the diplomatic life and dedicated the rest of his life to education, teaching Hispanic literature at Columbia University, Barnard College, and Middlebury College. He retired from academia in 1969, but continued to write poetry.

In 1982, he moved to Miami, where he resided until his death in 1994. While living in Florida, already in his eighties, he published two more collections of poetry: *Donde habite el recuerdo* (1984) and *Momentos* (1985). Florit also published numerous essays on varied topics, including literary criticism. While in Miami, he was accessible to younger poets and, health permitting, was willing to give readings and attend literary events. The poems included here were chosen by Florit before his death.

THE BABY GIRL

*N*ow you are among us, you really exist,
a tiny actuality of living blood,
still with some amazement,
uneasy still,
not knowing why you came.
(And you will never know,
although seraphs unfold
their wings to your gaze, although
God reveal Himself to you in a rose,
and the whole world yield itself to you in one evening.)
You will not know. And you will cry with grief,
and laugh, and wear your soul for all to see,
and love a pair of eyes,
and kiss the lips of life and death.
But you will not know.

Your journey here
is veiled in the mystery of music
that flows from star to star,
from sky to sky,
from heart to heart.
Your question comes
in you incarnate, with things
which we who watch you lack: the cloud you slept on,
your dream as an atom of light,
as a fleeting gleam of thought.
For I look at you and am afraid
to have you see my hardened soul,
you whose soul is so fragile, airy, pure, —
a little flame that scarcely bears
the yearning of more ardent fires.

And when you know that I watched you sleeping
and longed to ask you, when you woke,
the colour of your cloud,
the light in which you dreamed,
the thought you became in your sleep:
you will weep for me, who live
in this dream of absence, yearning
to go back to my cloud,
to my ray of light,
to my atom of earth:
to my permanent place in nothingness.

Translated by Donald Walsh.

ELEGY FOR YOUR ABSENCE

*I*n that moment you sailed for all of death
Into profound oceans of silence
With long hours of sleeping pupils,
And a flock of doves caught in your dreams.

Now you are already in distant moonlight,
More yourself than in the arrows of your golden clock
Where you reckoned such a shoreless moment
For the thirst of wings that was burning on your shoulders.

You shall have vaulted seas stared at by inquietude,
Abysses in the timid solitude of your absence;
And in the night you shall have been delicate warm breeze
Close to that crumb of your amorous earth.

Long embrace of breath over the poppies
And a laugh and a song without words or music;
With a "Here I am," glad of past wakefulness,
And a "forever" warm in the cool plain.

As you leave pressed in the arms of silence
The light of your words shall echo more clearly
And in each stanza of air an accent shall be entangled
And in each butterfly more wings shall be born to you.

Gladness of being alive for that eternal day,
Knowing yourself in the water, in the sun, and in the grass.
Among the clouds you shall make nativities of silver
And you shall discover your nest in a tree of stars.

Translated by H. R. Hays.

DEATH IN THE SUN

*T*he silent light penetrates the panes.
And in the mild air of this autumn,
Outside with the sun and the pigeons,
There is military music and solemn marching.
And within, in the clear silence,
We are so distant, ah, so lost,
That scarcely by the ticking of the clock
Do we remember that time exists.
And that it is a time of horror, a time of death
Over there where the light will be like this
And where, not like these, the pigeons die
In the poison of the winds,
And men meet their end.
And all is submerged in terror:
That terror of receiving death
On a sunny day
As sunny as this one,
With the silent light of this autumn.

Translated by H. R. Hays.

THE SIGNAL

*A*bove the laughter, Oh sea,
Above the delights of colors,
Above the blue and green stanza,
And above the white ribbon;
Above the yellow depth with the midday sun,
Above the night and above the gray locked under the sky,
Always the seagull

Rises and falls again from cloud to water
On outstretched wing and fleeting tenderness:
Spirit, gracious signal of the spirit,
Above the open laughter of the wave.

Translated by H. R. Hays.

AQUARIUM

Close to the sea — so far —
In lime and dead sand,
Imprisoned albatross, in a doze.
What yearning to fly over the foam
Of a free sea in hours of liberty!

Far — so near — their natural road,
People of keels and taut wings.
And the laughter, in sunlight, under the moon
Comes singing into the dry prison.

Here, for better or for worse,
Through fortune's avarice,
As an illusion of the highway,
In its core, this life
Of unhappy water, lonely fish,
Abandoned shell, empty of its dream.

All the light lost;
The tenderness of the sea, free to other ships,
In the clear kiss of the winds.

And, in the deep night, timidly, a sigh
For the open sea, for the brilliant foam,
By way of lime and dead sand.

Translated by H. R. Hays.

ANA ROSA NUÑEZ

*A*na Rosa Núñez (1926–) is a poet, literary critic, and librarian. She was born in Havana and studied at the Phillips Schools and the Baldor Academy. At the University of Havana, she received her doctorate in philosophy and literature in 1954, while simultaneously receiving a degree in library science, studies she continued both in Cuba and in exile in the United States.

She went into exile in 1965. Since then, she has resided in Miami, where she continues to write poetry and to work as a librarian at the University of Miami.

Several collections of Núñez' poetry have been published both in Cuba and abroad. Among these are *Siete lunas de enero, Viaje al cazabe, Sol de un solo día, Requiem para una isla, Hora doce,* and, most recently, *Crisántemos.* Her poems are also included in numerous anthologies and literary magazines.

In addition to her contributions as a poet, Ana Rosa Núñez has dedicated much of her life to the study of other writers. She has written several bibliographies and edited various anthologies. In addition, she works enthusiastically with young people, attempting to pass on her knowledge, as well as love of literature.

RESURRECTION

*P*ut me to death
in the blood of this crystal
that I might go unblemished to God.
An embrace of vineyards and sugarcane
overthrew the quietude in which I rose.
A sweet embrace remembered
will open into the light
the protected, ravelled way,
used for the first time
in centuries of brotherly silence.
Through so much anointing,
through so much stony silence
moist silence of tile sun of flight
— silence revived in cries.
Put me to death
in the mystery of Your wine and Your water
on the side through which I live,
on the rock in which I seek wisdom
through the fog of a mystical tropical morning.
If I am put to death this way
I might live forever in the silence
of a day without soil and brine.

Translated by José E. Fernández.

IMMUTABILITY

I am the voice for your song;
Bright bird
That announces the summer.
No one hears
In the modulations
Of your voice
The heraldic words
Of the blue flaming sun.
Your seasonal voice
Has fixed names on the earth.

There, in other galaxies
The heart of all creation explodes
(to create the uncreated)

Silence is the host
Of your immutability.
Have patience with the meanderers.
Take heart
There is in your song
The silhouette of the unexpected.
The defenseless tyranny
Hung between the ethereal
And the repetitive
The sun,
The earth,
The man,
The time
And the space.

October, 1983.

Translated by José E. Fernández.

BLACK HAIKU

*B*ecause we are all made of carbon
all of us have
the same color.

The day wakes up in white.
The night sleeps in black.
Dreams are mulatto.

In the life of the heron
blacks and whites
are united.

The ceiba tree has been
your goddess
in mystery and misery.

In the mamey's heart
there are miles and miles
of sugar factory batey.

The dead rise up
to the drum.
Because a mystic lives in its voice.

It snowed in the black man's skin
one night without secrets.

The drum appears
as a decapitated palm tree
that repeats good-bye, good-bye, good-bye.

In the blood of the coffee
is born since the beginning
mamá Inés.

From the black man that walks
and the white man that rests,
we are separated only by water.

Translated by Carolina Hospital.

JOSE YGLESIAS

José Yglesias (1919–1996) was born in Ybor City, in Tampa, of Cuban and Spanish parents. In his youth, Yglesias witnessed many of the changes that the Tampa Cuban enclave was undergoing in the late 1920s and 1930s. For example, he observed his mother's involvement in the 1931 cigarmakers' strike when the factory readers were forced out from the factories and replaced by radios. Although until recently, he lived in New York with his wife and family, Yglesias has emerged as a representative of the "Tampeño" writer. His writings often reflect an attachment to Tampa and Ybor City, where he grew up, as well as an interest in depicting the lives of working class Hispanics in the U.S.

Yglesias was educated at Black Mountain College in North Carolina and worked as a free-lance writer since 1963. He published several works, including *The Truth About Them* (1971), of which we have included an excerpt. He has also published *Awake in Ybor City* (1963), *Goodbye Land* (1967), *In the Fist of the Revolution: Life in a Cuban Country Town* (1968), *An Orderly Life* (1968), *The Franco Years* (1977), and several other books in both Spanish and English. In addition, he translated books by Juan Goytisolo and Xavier Domingo, and contributed extensively to national magazines such as *The New Yorker, New York Times Magazine, Esquire, Nation, New Republic,* and *New York Times Book Review,* to name a few.

THE TRUTH ABOUT THEM

*E*ven today Key West hides none of its flat terrain from those who approach it from the sea. Grandmother saw it for the first time, in 1890, from the New York steamer while it navigated the reefs along the southern shore. The deck of the ship placed her and Grandfather on a level with the few two-story buildings on the island, and she was able to take in most of it before stepping ashore. Especially the southwest corner, which the ship slowly rounded to reach the piers on the north shore. It was at the turn where the Latins working in the cigar industry lived. The island was no more than ten blocks wide at that spot, but it looked even smaller to Grandfather. He had last seen it when he was seventeen, eight years earlier. The sight delighted him — he could make out the pebbly shore where he had often played when he should have been at school — and because it appeared manageably little, it also reassured him. Not Grandmother; for her this was the start of a new life. Years later, she confided to her six grown daughters, "When I saw those rows of tiny unpainted houses to which your father pointed — aiee! my soul shriveled."

The oldest daughter was not Grandfather's. She was illegitimate. Early during that pregnancy, Grandmother left her sister's home in Cuba accompanied by a Negro couple, given to her at birth by her grandparents, and stopped in Nassau until Aunt Titi was born. From there she traveled with her former house slaves to New York. Then to Philadelphia, where she met Grandfather and was married by the Reverend W. R. Carroll, rector of the Episcopalian Church. Less than six months later, her second daughter (Grandfather's first) was born in Brooklyn. The Negro couple remained in Philadelphia, their job done, and Aunt Titi, who was eleven when they left New York, took care of her infant half-sister on the voyage to Key West, as she was to do with the others to come and their children for the rest of her life. Grandmother was again pregnant and she was sick from the moment the ship left its moorings. Sick with apprehension, perhaps. Her in-laws in Key West, whom she had never met, believed she was twenty-five, like Grandfather, but she was, in fact, thirty-five. They had been married less than two years; the honeymoon was over. She was irrevocably a cigarmaker's wife, and what was for Grandfather a happy return home looked to her like a further descent into the unknown world of the working class.

It has taken me almost a lifetime to gather these few truths about them (and others to be told at the proper time) and to arrange them in this order. These facts have haunted my life and that of my cousins. They do not seem much after so long a search. (Not that I was obsessed from day to day, but there is reason, God knows, to look in any direction, including back into time, for a happier way of living.) Recently, sitting on my mother's porch in Tampa, where my grandparents finally settled, I leafed through the century-old album that Grandmother had brought from Cuba. There she was, in that pristine time, among the photographs of beautiful young ladies from Matanzas and Havana, grouped in bouquets or alone in oval-shaped portraits posed in three-quarters profile, their eyes consciously veiled, chaste as cameos. A brass corner of the album loosened in my hand, and the green velvet it had covered emerged as fresh as a spring leaf.

I sighed and clapped the book shut with an effort, despairing of ever really knowing the life my grandmother had led. Boom! The sound of the closing book carried to the yard where Mother was watering the azaleas. She turned and looked at me — like a mother always on call — and shut off the hose. Her uncertain smile announced confidences all the way to my corner of the porch; so did the quick turns of her head to check if some neighbor could overhear. She leaned above me. "Pini!" she whispered. Behind her the giant oak sheltered us both.

I looked at her expectantly.

"Do you know that my mother never married Aunt Titi's father?"

"I know," I said.

"How?" she exclaimed, her voice strangled by the effort not to shout. "Who told you?"

"Cousin Zenaida," I said.

"Ah." Mother sighed, meaning she was glad the revelation had come from someone in the family. The fear that others outside the family might have known had been reflected one moment in her clear brown eyes. She turned away a second and thought about this, and it gave her the bashful look of the girls in the album. When she gazed at me again, she said, "Zenaida, of course," and I knew she meant that Zenaida had broken the rule of the Spanish-Cuban women of Tampa that men are not to be privy, except in unsmotherable crises, to family secrets. Mother sighed anew. Sadly this time. I had never seen her feel old until then.

"After Grandfather died," I explained. "That's when she told me."

"Yes, of course," she said, though she had not been at all sure about Zenaida's discretion. It made her feel better for Grandfather. That upright man. It took a car to knock him down when he was seventy-eight. In all those years there had never been any gossip to mar his sense of his life with Grandmother. Both of them were forgotten now outside the family, but Mother was still on the alert. Her decision to tell me must have been made on an impulse, and I could see her worry the thought that I had known for twenty-two years. She looked at me to search for that new person I had so long ago become. She saw a middle-aged man. We were equals. . . .

Those great secular funerals — they were the first to go. Or, rather, when their form began to change, when the dead were no longer laid out at home but at funeral parlors and it was there you went, for a few brief hours, to mourn and pay your respects, when that happened, it was already too late to reclaim Ybor City and West Tampa. They were mortally wounded and we didn't know it. Such a sensible change, particularly under the special circumstances of Aunt Titi's death three years later, why should it lead to a freeway cutting a swath through the community and to urban renewal bulldozers leveling block after block of wooden houses? You stand on the steps of the Cuban Club today and see all the way to Twenty-second Street, and the fuss that Mama Chucha raised about laying out Aunt Titi at a funeral parlor seems now full of prophecy. No one walks, not even on Seventh Avenue (only the Americans ever got to call it East Broadway) although the Chamber of Commerce has given it a center island with palms, and the sidewalks, once so crowded, have been decorated with iron grillwork that looks like plastic. Bad Negroes from Mississippi and Tennessee have moved into the old, termite-ridden houses, and the old men who still go to the clubs to play dominoes start home early so they will not be assaulted by one of them. I walked down Seventh Avenue the other day and a car slowed down alongside me and a voice called out, "What you doing here, man?" It belonged to a boy with whom I played marbles, and his face appeared streaked, puffed, and drained of color.

I almost asked what had happened to him.

Aunt Titi was not, indeed, laid out at a funeral parlor. My aunts and mother had planned it that way when they left New York with her body on a train called the Silver Meteor, having been urged to do so by their husbands and children, all adults and working in perfume factories and cafeteria kitchens in Manhattan. But Mama Chucha had never left Tampa. She, Papa Leandro, and the younger children survived the Depression on relief and the money orders that Cuco and the other boys in New York sent each week. Unlike the rest of us who had gravitated to New York, Mama Chucha had never seen a Jewish newspaper, a Chinese restaurant, the morning twenty-five-cent show at the Paramount; she had never sat in a subway underground and been hurtled — suddenly, astoundingly — into the open air to ride alongside the tops of buildings and see beyond them the Hudson River and, out the opposite windows, the dark valley of Harlem. Mama Chucha had not felt that little click inside her — like the uncoupling of noiseless trains — that separates one from the ways of West Tampa and Ybor City.

She screamed when she learned at the railroad station in Tampa that Aunt Titi's body was not going directly home.

"I shall take my sister to my home," she announced.

"What a thing to say!" Aunt Angela said. "Anyway, Titi has been dead three days."

"The more reason, the more reason," Mama Chucha said. "My home is not too fine for Titi's smell."

"Oh, oh!" Aunt Lulu turned to my mother. "Did you hear her! If Mama heard — "

"What do you think she would say?" Mama Chucha asked. "And Titi — what would she say? My sister who helped me with all my children and my broken arm, they want to treat her like a parcel now!"

Mother was unimpressed. "Titi was our sister too and it was we who gave her a home."

"Americans, that is what you are," Mama Chucha yelled. "Florida crackers. Without feelings. I am the oldest now and she is going to my home."

Mama Chucha won.

ANGEL CUADRA

*A*ngel Cuadra (1931–) is a poet and human rights activist. He was born in Havana, Cuba, where he studied theater and diplomacy at the University of Havana. He graduated as a lawyer in 1956, before the government closed the institution because of political turmoil. Cuadra was one of the students to publicly oppose the Batista dictatorship; he recited his poem "Lamento a José Martí en su centenarío" on the steps of the University of Havana in 1953. Five years later, this poem won him the prize of the Association of Ibero-American Poets of New York.

In 1959, Cuadra published his first book of poems, *Peldaño*. He continued to write and publish in secret after Castro took power until, in 1967, he was arrested for opposing the government. After serving nine years of his sentence, he was released in 1976; however, he was arrested once more for having published another book of poems — *Impromptus* — in the United States. The world outcry after his reimprisonment, and the further publication of another collection, *A Correspondence of Poems,* caused him to be transferred to a remote Cuban prison to serve solitary confinement. After serving his full fifteen-year sentence, Cuadra was released in 1982. He was not allowed to leave the island until 1985, and then only as a result of personal appeals to Fidel Castro by the Swedish and West German ambassadors.

Cuadra has resided in Miami since his departure. In exile, he continues to publish and give poetry readings. He also teaches as an adjunct professor both at Florida International University and at Miami-Dade Community College. He has received numerous literary awards for his poetic works and actively promotes the works of other Hispanic writers through his coordination at the Miami Book Fair International. In 1994, the University Presses of Florida published a collection of Cuadra's poems and essays in English translation, edited by Warren Hampton, entitled *The Poet in Socialist Cuba.*

BRIEF LETTER TO
DONALD WALSH
(IN MEMORIAM)

(Translator of my poems)

*M*y friend:
In what language shall we begin our conversation?
How can I begin to celebrate
the support your voice gives me
in sending out my songs, drenched in your accents,
to live in this world?
And not know what the warmth of your hand is like in
friendship;
only this music shining from the soul,
stretching like a bridge between us:
you in your country open to the stars,
I behind bars of rancor,
dying since the dawn.
Yet even so we meet.
The hands of friends
brought your name to me with the morning dew.
And you are here, and I am talking to you.

Because I've learned that not everything is hatred.
I want to declare another word,
sow it as it were in furrows
of goodness and of hope.

There are some men who crush my words,
tear me to pieces for producing beauty,
bring my poem to trial
and sentence it to run the gauntlet:
the drops of blood my poem sheds
form a constellation among the stars.

But there are other men who rescue me
and save my poem like unransomed light,
who gather up its pieces of suffering clay
and, like Prometheus, lend me fire for it.
The fire of love, I proclaim it now,
that is the word I will defend
in martyrdom, among the thorns.
My poem, the grape of pain
for which I bleed and grow.
And you exist, Donald Walsh.
I knew nothing of your musical being,
of that gemstone clear and high, transparent.
Don't leave now
that I have found days dawning in my heart
that were sent me by your hand.
Don't leave now
that we begin to speak in a language
that unites the souls of Whitman and Martí.
And on the streets of all the world
—without bars, without bitterness or fear
—you and I will walk together, speaking
the word of Love that has existed since before the age of man.

Translation by Catherine Rodríguez-Nieto.

(Donald Walsh died a few days before the arrival of this poem,
which was enclosed with a letter written in April, 1980.)

REPEATED THEME

*N*ight has fallen, it is raining . . .
How many times has this been said before;
the same nostalgia spoken of,
or the same sadness
like a song repeated in the rain
in the same key.
Nothing new.

But this music of water
is falling now outside,
and inside me.
Verlaine said once, "Il pleut dans mon coeur,"
And it is raining here too, now, in my heart.
Life is raining,
everything that ever fell is raining
(my collapse, my masts to the wind),
all that might have been, like history,
and that one time . . .
Ah, time, my enemy,
always appearing on my daily account,
in the absurdity of living that has been
like steady rain in my hourglass.

Tonight, like all those others,
away from you, I love you,
and in the rain falling outside
your name is singing too:
ah, the name of love
that has been invented to name you.
You are the rain of my life,
you slip away like water between my fingers.
You are a drink of rainwater,
sometimes bitter, when the rain of your absence is falling,

when you are the rainfall of your loss,
slipping away
into nothingness.
My little rain
that began falling slowly into my time,
always here,
inside my heart,
along my inner streets,
falling like this, falling on me
like drops of sky.
And my rain outside
for the thirst of all the universe.
My woman of rain,
wound of rain,
sorrow of rain,
joy of rain,
raining on me like tenderness,
like little bells of water;
my day of celebration;
breasts of rain,
mouth of rain,
eyes, hands, caress of rain;
unfamiliar rain as well . . .,
I have grown old loving you
on the roads of my existence
beset by impossible rains,
threatened always by your absence of rain,
hopeful always
of the coming of your rain as well.

Night has fallen, it is raining . . .
I am saying these things today,
just as others said them yesterday.

Translated By Catherine Rodríguez-Nieto.

IN BRIEF

*T*he common man I might have been
reproaches me now,
blaming me for his ostracism
his solitary shadow,
his silent exile.

I put my common man and the other man together.
I took the latter's hand and moved away,
as if to honor my brilliant friend,
my wished-for double,
my important, chosen self.
And the common man I told
to shut the door behind him,
to be quiet behind the panes,
or rather, to give up his place in the window
and, if possible, to wipe away his image with a cloth.

Time passed in its hurried way,
planetary time that is,
or simply,
the time spent on the road.

I have retraced my footsteps now —
with my other, my own self —
not sure if I am proud or sad.
It has rained on my face,
many nights have fallen.
Above the dust only one cold star
that seems like dust itself, like the mute dust
I brought back with me.
And I find my common man still there,
where I left him, the one I denied,
the unimportant man I might have been;

and in his eyes of exile I can see
a stupor of sand and time and emptiness.
I look then at the other, the important man,
the one I chose to be.
I put my common man and the other man together . . .
and find they are one and the same.

Translated by Catherine Rodríguez-Nieto.

HEBERTO PADILLA

H *eberto Padilla* (1932–) is a poet and essayist. Many have called him the most important poet of the Spanish language today. He was born in Pinar del Rio, Cuba, in 1932. From a young age, he was interested in both literature and social issues. In 1948, at only sixteen years of age, he finished his first poetry manuscript, *Las rosas audaces*. He was also involved in journalism; the decade of the 1950s was filled with political turmoil which called his attention to social and political issues. In 1957, during the Batista dictatorship, he went into exile in New York and Miami, where he attended the University of Miami. Soon after Castro took power in 1959, Padilla returned to the island with hope and idealism for the future.

During the early 1960s, he occupied several posts as correspondent and cultural attaché abroad. During this time, he published two more collections of poetry: *El justo tiempo humano* and *La hora*. By 1968, however, his book *Fuera del juego* had thrust him in the middle of a political crisis. Even though the book was published and acclaimed, its critical attitude toward the development of the revolution resulted in his arrest in 1971. His imprisonment, along with his wife, poet Belkis Cuza Malé (whom he had married in 1966), and his forced self-denunciation created such an international scandal, among the European intellectuals in particular, that it became known as "The Padilla Affair." This event was viewed as a betrayal of artistic and cultural freedoms and marked a drastic change of perception abroad toward the revolution.

Padilla was quickly released due to international pressure, but he was never allowed to work or publish again. He dedicated his time to translations until he was finally granted permission to leave the island in 1980. Since then, he has lived in Princeton, New Jersey, and Miami, where he currently lives with his family.

Since his return to exile, he has published several books: two bilingual collections of poetry, *Legacies: Selected Poems* and *A Fountain, A House of Stone: Poems*; the novel *Heroes are Grazing in My Garden*; and a memoir, *Self-Portrait of the Other*. In addition, he has given numerous courses at universities throughout the U.S., including Florida International and the University of Miami. In addition, he publishes weekly editorials in *El Nuevo Herald* in Miami and in other newspapers nationally and abroad.

TO BELKIS, WHEN SHE PAINTS

*W*hile she paints she always tilts her head
to the same side
to let the colors come out, she says,
truest and brightest.
But she doesn't know I watch and see her transfigured.
Her hair is long and straight and I braid it as I want,
it's black and I redden it until it throbs like a burn,
I raise her hands from the painting
and make them part of the blaze.
I like to imagine her everywhere,
ubiquitous, ghostly,
filling the whole convulsed map of my poems.
Example:
            dressed in a cashmere sweater
Example:
            naked on the edge of a yellow beach
            like the cracked canvas of a Van Gogh
Example:
            in a canoe, looking for Isolde's magnolia
            for our wedding
Example:
            singing:
she and her solitude
she and the lamp above, she and the curtains
flowered by her hair;
joyous and uncombed
like an idle queen, in green, in red, in mauve
next to me, in her dark palmist's corner,
with my hand in her hand,
reading my palm to arm me against enemies.
Everywhere she everywhere
her black hair glowing through the smoke
from the bowl of my coral pipe.

Translated by Alistair Reid and Andrew Hurley.

IN TRYING TIMES

*T*hey asked that man for his time
so that he could link it to History.
They asked him for his hands,
because for trying times
nothing is better than a good pair of hands.
They asked him for his eyes
that once had tears
so that he should see the bright side
(the bright side of life, especially)
because to see horror one startled eye is enough.
They asked him for his lips, parched and split, to affirm,
to belch up, with each affirmation, a dream
(the great dream);
they asked him for his legs
hard and knotted
(his wandering legs),
because in trying times
is there anything better than a pair of legs
for building or digging ditches?
They asked him for the grove that fed him as a child,
with its obedient tree.
They asked him for his breast, heart, his shoulders.
They told him
that that was absolutely necessary.
They explained to him later
that all this gift would be useless
unless he turned his tongue over to them,
because in trying times
nothing is so useful in checking hatred and lies.
And finally they begged him,
please, to go take a walk.
Because in trying times
that is, without a doubt, the decisive test.

Translated by Alistair Reid and Andrew Hurley.

SOMETIMES I PLUNGE

*S*ometimes I plunge into the ocean, for a long time,
and emerge suddenly gasping, breathing,
and swim as far as I can from the coast
and see the distant blurred line of the shore
and the sun making the oily water boil.
The shoreline drowns in the vapor
and I close my eyes blinded by the light.
Then, a handsbreadth from those waves, the country appears
that for so long we thought
we were carrying on our shoulders: white, like a warship,
shining against the sun and against poets.

Translated by Alistair Reid and Andrew Hurley.

MARTHA PADILLA

M artha Padilla (1938?–) is a poet born in Pinar del Rio, where she did her studies and began her literary endeavors. While still an adolescent, she published her first book of poems, *Comitiva al Crepúsculo,* and later *Modos del Pan.* She began her university studies, but these were abruptly interrupted when her family, including her brother poet Heberto Padilla, moved to Miami in 1957, a few years before the Revolution.

In exile, her first literary success was the book *Alborada del Tigre.* In Miami and Puerto Rico, she continued to publish several books of poetry, including *Los Tiros del Mísere, El Fin del Tiempo Injusto,* and *Nuestro Gustavo Becquer.* Her book *La Pareja* received the Spanish Prize La Carabela de Oro. In 1973, she won the Cintas Fellowship in Literature. For many years, she participated actively in round tables, conferences, readings, and debates, while continuing to publish in anthologies. In 1984, she moved to Marietta, Georgia, where she currently lives, dedicated to her poetry and her family. Recently, she published some of her newest work in *Perfil de Frente*, a limited edition published in Arlington, Virginia.

V

*M*rs. E. Roosevelt
Was the first heroine
In my stay in this world
With her ugly
And gracious American countenance
Full of love and tears
She summoned the lights
For the Conference at Yalta
And maybe
Even wrote with her smile
White, in the Black Sea
Who knows . . .
I was a child
With all the innocence
Of a girl
During the years of the last war.

Translated by Carolina Hospital.

X

*T*hen
In the Wax Museum
I discovered my silhouette
I discovered my breasts of motherhood
I discovered my penitent decorum
I discovered myself
In the block across the street
Walking towards the oval
Of the smile
Puzzled
I discovered my skeleton dressed in green
And my city submerged in its blood.

Translated by Carolina Hospital.

MARTHA PADILLA

EXPOSITION SEPIA

I have spent my life
sleeping in other doors
eating in other plates, drinking in other faucets

I have ridden my colt with unfamiliar reins
I have buried myself in the sand of an orphaned beach

Like a top I have danced for myself always
And in the ruins I have been, the one who erases the dates

Translated by Carolina Hospital.

HILDA PERERA

*H*ilda Perera (1926–   ) was born in Havana. She began her literary career at the age of seventeen with the publication of the collection of stories *Cuentos de Apolo*. In 1948, she obtained a one-year scholarship to Western College for Women in Ohio, where she completed a Bachelor of Arts degree. Back in Havana, she received her Ph.D. from the University of Havana.

She was involved in education in Havana, serving as the director of the Spanish Department in Ruston Academy, as a course planning counselor for the National Library, and as an educational counselor in the Cuban National Commission of UNESCO. She published several grammar and reading textbooks. In addition to her educational endeavors in Cuba and in Miami, where she has lived since 1964, she continued to publish both children's literature and novels.

Her novels include *Mañana es 26*, about the insurrectional struggle against Batista; the bestseller in Spain, *El sitio de nadie*, which was a finalist in The International Prize for Poetry sponsored by Planeta Press in 1972; *Felices Pascuas*; *Plantado*; *Los Robledal*; and, most recently, *La Noche de Ina*.

Perera is also well known for her children's books, including several collections of stories and two novels, *Mai* and *Kike,* the latter of which has been translated into English and has enjoyed wide popularity in both languages. An excerpt from *Kike* is included here. The book deals with Cuban-American children sent into exile alone and the adventures they encounter as they adapt to their new environment.

When Perera left Cuba in 1964, she moved to Miami and received a Master of Arts degree from the University of Miami. She continues to reside in Miami with her two children and numerous grandchildren. She participates actively in the Miami literary life, often giving readings and lectures on a variety of topics.

KIKE

VII

Paco

In winter the Everglades would fill up with hunters who came in on swamp buggies, trucks with huge fat tires that won't sink in the muck. they brought long shotguns and dogs that pause and smell the air to find the deer.

Once, a Cuban doctor with enough money to spend on guns and bullets invited Juanito and me to go along on a hunt. He taught me how to shoot. He also had some very expensive hunting dogs. Juanito told me they even sent the dogs to special training schools where they were taught to hunt. I thought to myself that the money would be better spent on teaching children and not dogs. But I didn't say anything; I was having a good time and the doctor might not like it.

Early next morning the Cuban doctor roasted a young pig. We all sat around the barbeque pit and sang Cuban songs. It was a lot of fun until later, when the hunters shot a buck and bound his legs around a pole to carry him out of the swamp. The buck's eyes were open, and as they walked he left a trail of dripping blood.

I didn't like the men anymore, even if they were Cubans, like me. I decided that next time, before a hunt, Juanito and I would scare away all the deer. Juanito seemed to be reading my mind. He told me that there was an old lady from Miami who spent all her time fighting against deer hunting in the Everglades. Some people believe it's good to hunt deer to keep their numbers down. But the truth is that most of the hunters kill the animals just for the fun of it.

A lot of motorcycle gangs would also come to the Everglades. The riders wore black helmets, black leather jackets, and sunglasses like pilots in old World War II films. You could hardly see their faces. They all wore their hair long and mnay of the men had beards.

I found Paco thanks to the motorcycles. he was trying to cross the road, but it was dark and the motorcyclists didn't see him, so they ran over him. Juanito and I rescued him. We nursed him and put him in a cage.

Paco was a raccoon. I didn't know how to say raccoon in Spanish because I had never seen one in Cuba. By then I was learning the names for things in English that I had never known in Spanish. And it's been that way ever since. Juanito told me that the word for raccoon in Spanish is *mapache.*

Paco's forelegs looked like little human hands with fingernails. It was funny to see him hold a nursing bottle. Since Paco was still growing, Osceola told me to set him loose.

"Animals are not toys, Kiki," said Osceola.

He was wrong. Paco was a live toy for me. No one had given me anything to play with in this country, so I made up my mind to keep Paco.

But Osceola insisted that if I really cared for Paco I would turn him loose. Paco clung to my shirt with his sharp nails as if fearing that Osceola would convince me. Setting Paco loose worried me. I had grown fond of him, but perhaps Osceola was right.

"Look, Paco, we should listen to Osceola," I told him. "You're growing up and you must learn to be on your own. If you don't, you'll never grow up to be a free raccoon."

Finally, I opened the cage and said good-bye to Paco, thinking he would leave. But the next morning, he was back in the cage. Juanito and I then decided to carry him off where he couldn't find us, so he'd learn to be free.

We took Paco away during one of those airboat rides Mike gave the tourists. I got off with Paco on a little island where, according to Mike, there had once been a village of fierce Indians. Even though the Everglades was one big swamp, there were some higher, drier places, little islands known as hammocks. There, you wouldn't sink in the mud. It was on a hammock that I left Paco. I meant to leave him and return in a few days to check on him. As soon as Mike started the engine and we were ready to take off, poor Paco raised his snout and sniffed the air worriedly. It was as if he knew we were leaving him for good.

Just a day or so later, there was a big fire.

In the summer, it rains so much in the Everglades that everything floods and the place looks like one big lake. But during the winter it almost doesn't rain at all. Then, a fire can get started very easily: any small flame will set fire to the grass, which sets fire to a tree, and then another, and another and another, until everything burns. At night, sparks shoot up like fireworks. Sometimes the fires last for days. When they are over you see miles of burnt grass, ashes, and scorched trees.

As soon as I saw fire on the island where we left Paco, I called Juanito.

"Wake up! Wake up! There's a big fire outside and we've got to save Paco!"
"Ay, bendito!" Juanito said, jumping into his pants. Then, we called Tony.
Silently, the three of us left the house and got on one of the airboats. We rowed
quietly for a while, until we were far enough to start the engine without waking
Mike. When we got to the island we found poor Paco in a circle of flames. He was
dying of fright. I ran to rescue him.

"Don't go in, Kiki, don't be a fool!" Tony shouted.

But I jumped off anyway, and picked up Paco as fast as I could. On the way
out, my shirt caught fire. I rolled on the ground. Tony and Juanito threw a wet
blanket over me. But I got burnt anyway. When we got back Tony put oil and ice
over my blisters. They hurt.

From then on, I kept Paco in his cage with the door open. But he never left
it. The next time Osceola told me to set Paco free, I answered I couldn't force him
to leave if he didn't want to.

"It isn't right for people to live caged up against their will; but it isn't right
either for me to force Paco to live free against his will. Paco has the right to live
wherever he wants!" I argued.

Osceola smiled and scratched his head. I told him that there were lots of
people in the world who weren't free, like the Cubans who lived in Cuba, but
they had no choice. At least, in Paco's case, the cage door was open. In the
Cubans' case, it wasn't.

The next day after the fire, Mike got upset over the airboat. "Who the hell's
been playing with my boat?"

I still don't know how he found out. Maybe it was the way we tied it to the
pier. Mike was furious. He whipped out his belt and was on the point of giving us
a thrashing when Mama stood between him and us, pleading:

"Don't you dare, Mike! They'll take the kids away from us!"

ARMANDO ALVAREZ BRAVO

*A*rmando *Alvarez Bravo* (1938–   ) was born in Havana. He grew up in different neighborhoods of Havana, including La Habana Vieja and El Vedado, and New York. He became interested in literature at a young age under the tutelage of his mother, Ana María. He also shared much time with the renowned Cuban writer José Lezama Lima, one of the few Cuban writers of his time who never left the island. After years of isolation and silence under the Castro government, Alvarez Bravo went into exile in Miami.

In exile, he has continued to publish books of essays and poetry, including *Para domar un animal, Juicio de residencia, El prisma de la razón*, and *Naufragios y comentarios*. He has won numerous awards for his poetry and is currently editing several volumes of Cuban literature. In addition to his own creative work, Armando Alvarez Bravo maintains a strong presence in Miami in his role as editor and columnist in *El Nuevo Herald's* arts section.

Exile is a predominant theme in Bravo's texts. His work emerges from a sense of loss to search for innocence through beauty and meditation. He often explores cultural, historical, and ethical issues as well.

NOTATIONS

1/Notation

a rough day
and a quiet dinner
(all by myself)
best course
      conversation

three letters from Cuba
dreadful news

a tired
      helpless
lonely man

sadness depression

keep the colous flying!

2/Sentences

noon
the endless wait
a crowded lonely place
just one more brandy won't kill me
yesterday the past was a strange conversation piece
the bitter taste of an unknown victory
a weak heart and a lust for life
untold words and feelings
keep smiling
the bloody game you've got to play
old pros don't cry
a thing of beauty is a joy . . .

let's take a chance
I think this is much more than the beginning
          of a beautiful friendship
got to go
miss you
have gun will travel
but you know.

3/An early Autumn Briefing

work
          drink
and smoke yourself to death
find no rest
find no love
dreams are forbidden here
everybody will approve
if you just behave
that's your neglected duty
the taming is on us.

4/Findings

lost family
lost country
lost loves
lost dreams
lost you name it
lost losses-

a total loss.

5/Portrait of the Artist as a Still Life

a Smith & Wesson
a Smith-Corona
some faded pictures
a battered old radio
a bottle of Scotch
an empty pack of cigarettes
the ultimate etcetera
on a messy desk
that outgrows
a circle of yellow light

(the painting is dated
December 1989
it is fifty years old
almost an antique)

PURA DEL PRADO

*P*ura del Prado (1931–   ) is a poet, teacher, and journalist born in Santiago. In Cuba, she was a teacher as well as an active member of numerous literary and pedagogical organizations. Since her exile in 1958, before the Cuban revolution, she has traveled extensively throughout Europe, living for many years in Paris. She became a United States citizen in 1963, and currently lives in Miami Beach.

As a poet, she has received many literary awards, including the Cuban National Prize in Poetry, the Jorge Mañach Prize, and the Lincoln Martí Poetry Prize. She has given numerous poetry readings, and her poems have appeared frequently in poetry anthologies published in Cuba, Argentina, Italy, Spain, Holland, and Miami.

Her books include *De codos en el arco iris*, *Los sábados de Juan Pérez*, *Canto a Martí*, and *El río con sed*, all published in Cuba. In exile, she has published *Nuestro Gustavo Adolfo Becquer* (in collaboration with Martha Padilla, Ana Rosa Núñez, and Josefina Inclán), *La otra orilla*, *Otoño enamorado*, and *Idilio del Girasol*.

AN EXILE'S MONOLOGUE

*M*iami resembles Cuba
but without *yenyere*
nor red tiles
nor the smell of sugarcane juice
nor those black men
oh those black men,
so different.
It's missing, I don't know what,
the most delicious things:
an unpacked mamey,
two or three hills,
the bus, the *guaguancó*,
played with a golden tooth smile
on an old box of beer.
And the beaches without wounds on my feet.
Those colors of water and sky,
of sand and cloud,
do not resemble each other,
they are not twins.
The shade waiting for transportation,
the chicken raised in the backyard,
which ate even the smallest bone.
We have trapped the *décima* in disco,
it no longer trots in the field,
the Cathedral Plaza,
it is aimless in the cabaret,
a dead decoration.
Cecilia Valdés sings
that she is a jingle bell and a church bell,
with anguished and nostalgic eyes.
The conga dancers
full of a people,
are hardly a copy

of club dancers.
Even Olga Guillot
has changed us
and in the depth of her sensuality
there is a coarseness, a timid sob.
Celia Cruz looks like
Celia Cruz
and Portabales
transports us to our rooster buddy
without feathers and cackling.
Eighth Street
is an attempt at recuperating goods,
but it doesn't stop being a graft.
They have remodeled
the *Virgen del Cobre*,
its pebbles strange with golden streaks,
cool hills,
a room of miracles.
Santa Barbara emigrated
with her apples and pennies,
and her sword is inactive,
so she doesn't get arrested in Nassau.
We Cubans
tell of our calamities
and blame each other for the root of our troubles
as if we lacked our own soil.
The Zig Zag makes fun
entertaining the "until when"
and the desperation
turns into bursts of laughter.
We can't complain,
we lack nothing,
the freezer is full,
the plates steam,
there is no heat in June;
but my friends,
we miss even the flies

protected by the screens.
The television consoles us
with a roundtable to vent our frustrations,
and on the streets a funeral-like
silence,
makes us evoke the noise,
the serenades without denunciations to the police,
the block parties,
the last chance of the night.
But Matías Vega has already died.
The *Bolita* lies in hiding
without glass cases nor poems
about the animal which runs on the roofs
and throws out the elephant.
The naturalized soul
chews English
and the frita has moved over
to let the hamburger in.
But indeed, we argue,
curse each other
— my group and yours —
and each one of us has his own story,
his dead person, his grudge,
his radio station,
his newspaper.
Of course, we couldn't
transform ourselves completely.
But how I wish that I could return to my garden,
that exile would end,
that my inventory would be returned,
that agrarian reform would be unraveled,
that I could hang up my old paintings,
take out my books, my spoons,
my Seawall, my Home.

Translated by Carolina Hospital.

GRANDMOTHER

*L*eonor, the sweet black laundress,
a pure woman with a simple loneliness,
taught me to spell in my primer
and to breathe deeply in Spring.

Among her almond trees, in the clay
she had fireflies and a beehive.
And in her tiny wooden house
I learned to kiss her cheek.

Leonor wore small golden earrings
and stored in a trunk, like a treasure,
postcards filled with all her tenderness.

Because of her, my heart is *mestizo*.
I love the pain of curly hair
and the sadness of her dark skin.

Translated by Carolina Hospital.

JUANA ROSA PITA

*J*uana Rosa Pita (1939–) is a poet who was born in Havana. In 1961, she left Cuba and since then has lived in Washington, Caracas, Boston, Madrid, and Miami, where she currently resides. From 1976 to 1986, she directed Solar poetry editions. She has written numerous collections of poetry; her most recent works include *Arie etrusche/ Aires etruscos*, published after receiving the international prize ALGHERO "Culture for Peace"; *Plaza sitiada*, the first volume of the collection "Poetry in Exile" directed by Pablo Antonio Cuadra; and *Sorbos de luz/ Sips of Light*.

Laurated in Spain and Italy, her work has been translated into English, German, and Italian, and included in anthologies of contemporary literature such as *New Directions in Prose* and *Poetry 49* in New York. She taught at various universities, including Tulane University in New Orleans. She recently received the Letras de Oro Award, sponsored by the University of Miami.

SIPS OF LIGHT

2

On sighting the sun anew
I wanted to greet him
but my voice had shattered.

11

As the fisherman leaves
under the twilight his net
I'll let fall my poem.

34

The fingers on their hands,
hands to their piano
sprouting its own music.

42

After the rain, magnolia
trees proclaim to heaven
what the river was hushing.

54

Orchids find fault
if violets dream
with seas of the North.

Translated by Mario de Salvatierra.

BELKIS CUZA MALE

$\mathcal{B}$*elkis Cuza Malé* (1942–) is a poet, essayist, and biographer. She was born in Guantánamo, Cuba. Because of her zeal for writing at a young age, her working-class parents made great efforts to sent her to private schools. Eventually, she attended the University of Oriente and earned the equivalent of a master's degree in literature.

By then, she had already received recognition by Casa de las Américas, in 1962 and in 1963, for her first two collections of poems: *Tiempos del sol* and *Cartas a Ana Frank*. After her graduation in 1964, she moved to Havana and worked as a radio and television critic for the newspaper *Hoy*. She also worked for *Granma* as editor of the cultural pages from 1966 to 1968, and wrote for the literary journal *La gaceta de Cuba*, published by UNEAC.

In 1966, Cuza Malé married poet Heberto Padilla. Five years later, in 1971, both were arrested by the government for diversionist writings. Even though, thanks to international pressure, both were soon released, their lives were changed forever. Cuza Malé's manuscript *Juego de Damas* had been a finalist for a Casa de las Américas prize in 1968. Already in press at the time of her arrest, the books were immediately shredded by censors as they were completed. She was never allowed to publish again. Her work, well recognized outside of the island by then, continued to be published in anthologies and journals abroad.

Malé was finally allowed to leave the island in 1979 and has lived in exile in the United States since then, in Princeton, New Jersey, Miami, and most recently Texas. Since her exile, she has published four books: *El Clavel y La Rosa*, a biography of the Cuban poet and artist Juana Borrero; *Woman on the Front Lines*, a bilingual selection of poems from different unpublished manuscripts, and the nonfiction books *Elvis or The True Story of Jon Burrows* and *In Search of Selena*. She has several manuscripts of poetry, two novels, a memoir, and a biography of

Gertrudis Gómez de Avellaneda still waiting to find publishers. She also writes a weekly column in *El Nuevo Herald* in Miami.

In addition to her own writing, Cuza Malé has worked diligently at promoting the works of other writers. She has done this primarily through her dedication to the literary magazine *Linden Lane,* now in its twelfth year. She edits the magazine from her home.

WOMEN DON'T DIE ON THE FRONT LINES

*W*omen don't die on the front lines,
their heads don't roll like golf balls,
they don't sleep under a forest of gunpowder,
they don't leave the sky in ruins.
No snow freezes their hearts.
Women don't die on the front lines,
they don't drive the devil out of Jerusalem,
they don't blow up aqueducts or railroads,
they don't master the arts of war or of peace either.
They don't make generals
or unknown soldiers carved out of stone
in town squares.
Women don't die on the front lines.
They are statues of salt in the Louvre,
mothers like Phaedra,
lovers of Henry the Eighth,
Mata Haris,
Eva Perons,
queens counselled by prime ministers,
nursemaids, cooks, washerwomen,
romantic poets.
Women don't make History,
but at nine months they push it out of their bellies
then sleep for twenty-four hours
like a soldier on leave from the front.

Translated by Pamela Carmell.

THE SILVER PLATTER

*T*his afternoon I've brought with me a silver platter.
I don't know what I'll do with it;
I've never had one before.
We live without these luxuries and you ask me:
"Do they still sell those things?"

No one pressures you to have silver platters.
Not even secondhand.
Who could, these days?
It's enough to have good table manners
and nice nails.
Some things, like saying grace, are out of style.

It's better to live without those luxuries,
not to want a poor man's salad
on a silver platter.

Translated by Pamela Carmell.

MY MOTHER'S HOMELAND

*M*y mother always said
your homeland is any place,
preferably the place where you die.
That's why she bought the most arid land,
the saddest landscape,
the driest grass, and beside the wretched tree
began to build her homeland.
She built it by fits and starts
      (one day this wall, another day the roof;
from time to time, holes to let air squeeze in).
My house, she would say, is my homeland,
and I would see her close her eyes
like a young girl full of dreams
while she chose, once again, groping,
the place where she would die.

Translated by Pamela Carmell.

AMANDO FERNANDEZ

A mando Fernández (1949–1994) was a poet and teacher, born in Havana in 1949. At the age of eleven, he left for Spain, where he resided for twenty years. In 1980, he moved to Miami, where he received his M.S. and M.A. from Florida International University. He taught for several years at Miami-Dade Community College's Interamerican Center and was actively involved in promoting the literary arts in the community. He died in Miami in 1994, after a long illness.

He is the author of several books of poetry, among them *El ruiseñor y la espada*, which won the Luis de Góngora Award (Diputacíon Provincial de Cordoba, Spain, 1989), *Materia y forma*, which won the Ciudad de Bandajoz Award (Diputacíon Provincial de Bandajoz, Spain, 1990) and *Los siete círculos*, which won the Antonio González de Lama Award (Ayuntamiento de Leon, Spain, 1991). He received numerous other awards abroad: Mairena, José María Heredia, Agustín Acosta, Jaen de poesía, and Odon Betanzos. He was also the recipient of the Oscar B. Cintas Fellowship awarded in the United States.

Amando Fernández was a prolific writer and dedicated his life to developing his own work, as well as encouraging others to revere poetry as much as he did.

THE FOREIGNER

*A*nd you, when your attested-to pride would be oblivion,
    rumor of litany, scarce earth,
to whom will you attend? who will prostrate the silence before
    your steps to lie your lie?
where the forgiveness of a mother's womb, the unreal and mythical
    patience, or the disaffection that you hear?
The pact of your body is brittle. Do not tell names.
    Nor forbidden or frustrated inclemencies.
Your return is lethargy, hard fatherland that announces last wills,
    flower in mourning.
Continue and do not watch behind you. Do not watch.
The voracious fire approaches the ramparts. Gird yourself well.
    Crown your forehead. Now your emptiness concludes.

Translated by David Miller.

DESCENT TO AGONY

You can give nothing because you have nothing:
neither a piece of white bread for hunger nor a place joined to the fire
    that heats the flesh
of one that advances in the cold of the night,
neither fresh water that would calm the other's thirst,
nor flowers that would make forget the heavy and corrupt air of the
    man who dies.
Your truth is near you and you would wish to offer a bloodless
    sacrifice, an intimate holocaust,
to the God who guards your minutes.
Your earth has remained of the silence of the thistle:
neither the lowest reptile, nor unwanted animals, make a nest.
You would not expect the miracle of the opportune rain
that would save you from being that which you are:
sandy dust, space without prodigy,
lesson and essay of elegy.
That which you have you know that is just;
for this, you have nothing.
But arrange your altar, kindle the fire, execute the appropriate
    rites.
And sacrifice the victim.

Translation by David Miller.

SALVATIO MUNDI

*O*bserving the things we discover the hope
and a hidden smile, almost quivering.
Upon watching them — with a certain immodesty if there is
innocence —
they are abandoned or are lived
depending upon the eyes and the angle
with which the sensitive man is delivered.
And if we approach
to expose ourselves to the wound of their just dimensions
we could perceive some profiles of candor
from their growing light,
a certain oracle, as of serene bounty, in their sustained
instants,
as awaiting a slight insinuation to offer their name,
their inseparable dignity
and better silence.
Understanding them is not important:
their transmutation is what saves you.

Translation by David Miller.

VIRGIL SUAREZ

Virgil Suárez (1962–   ) is a novelist, poet, and editor. He was born in Havana. In 1970, he traveled to Madrid, Spain, where he lived for the next four years. He then moved to Los Angeles, California, where he grew up and attended public school. He has a B.A. from California State University at Long Beach and an M.F.A. from Louisiana State University. He also studied with Sir Angus Wilson, Edward Abhey, Robert Houston, and Vance Bourjaily at the University of Arizona in Tucson for one year.

He currently lives with his family in Tallahassee, Florida, where he is an assistant professor in the Creative Writing Program at Florida State University. He teaches contemporary American literature, Latino/a Literature, and Latin American Literature. Recently he has become the fiction editor of *International Quarterly*.

He is the author of three published novels: *Latin Jazz, The Cutter,* and *Havana Thursdays*, as well as a collection of stories entitled *Welcome to the Oasis*. He is co-editor of the anthologies *Iguana Dreams: New Latino Fiction; Paper Dance: 55 Latino Poets*; and *Little Havana Blues*.

Suarez is currently working on several projects, including two novels, *Going Under: A Cuban-American Fable* and *Sonny Manteca's Blues*, and a collection of poems and prose poems entitled *Spared Angola: Scars From a Cuban-American Childhood*, some of which have already appeared in national literary magazines.

BITTERNESS

*M*y father brings home the blood of horses on his hands, his rough, calloused, thick-fingered hands; he comes home from the slaughterhouse where the government puts him to kill old useless horses that arrive from all over the island. On his hands comes the blood encrusted and etched on the prints and wrinkles of his fingers, under his nails, dark with the dirt too, the filth and grime, the moons of his fingers pinked by the residue, his knuckles skinned from the endless work. Sticky and sweet scented is the blood of these horses, horses to feed the lions in the new zoo which is moving from Havana to Lenin's Park near where we live. Dark blood, this blood of the horses my father slaughters daily to feed the zoo lions. I, being a child, ask how many horses it takes to feed a single lion. This, of course, makes my father laugh. I watch as he washes and rinses the dried-up blood from his forearms and hands, those hands that kill the horses, the hands that sever through skin and flesh and crush through bone because tough is the meat of the old horses. Feed for the lions. So my father, the dissident, the *gusano*, the Yankee lover, walks to and from work on tired feet, on an aching body. He no longer talks to anybody, and less to us, his family. My mother and my grand-mother; his mother. But they leave him alone, to his moods, for they know what he is being put through. A test of will. Determination. Salvation and survival. My father, under the tent on the grounds of the new zoo, doesn't say much. He has learned how to speak with his hands. Sharp are the cuts he makes on the flesh. The horses are shot on the open fields, a bullet through the head, and are then carted to where my father, along with other men, do the butchering. He is thirty (the age I am now) and tired and when he comes home his hands are numb from all the chopping and cutting. This takes place in 1969.

Years later when we are allowed to leave Cuba and travel to Madrid - to the cold winter of Spain, we find ourselves living in a hospice. The three of us in a small room. (My grandmother died and was buried in Havana.) My father, my mother, and I and next door is a man named Izquierdo who keeps us awake with his phlegmy coughs. From the other side of the walls, his coughing sounds like thunder. We try to sleep; I try harder but the coughing seeps through and my father curses under his breath. I listen to the heat as it tic-tacs coming through the furnace. My father tries to make love to my mother. I try now not to listen. The mattress springs sound like bones crushing. My mother refuses without saying a word. This is the final time she does so tonight. There is what seems like an interminable silence, then my father breaks it by saying to my mother, "If you don't, I'll look for a Spanish woman who will." Silence again, then I think I hear my mother crying. *"Alguien,"* my father says, "Will want to, to . . ." And I lay there on my edge of the mattress, sweat coming on from the heat. My eyes are closed and I listen hard and then the sound of everything stops. This, I think, is the way death must sound. Then my father begins all over again. The room fills with the small sounds . . . the cleaver falls and cuts through the skin, tears through the flesh, crushes the bone, and then there is the blood. All that blood. It emerges and collects on the slaughter tables, the blood of countless horses. Sleep upon me, I see my father stand by the sink in the patio of the house in Havana. He scrubs and rinses his hands. The blood dissolves slowly in the water. Once again I build up the courage to go ahead and ask him how much horsemeat it takes to appease the hunger of a single lion.

GUSTAVO PEREZ-FIRMAT

*G*ustavo *Pérez-Firmat* (1949–) is a poet, essayist, and literary critic. He was born in Havana and raised in Miami. He studied at the University of Miami and received his Ph.D. in comparative literature at the University of Michigan. Currently, he teaches at Duke University. He is well known for his books of literary criticism which include *Idle Fictions, Literature and Liminality, The Cuban Condition*, and *Life on the Hyphen*. In addition, he has published extensively in literary magazines in the United States and Spain. Furthermore, he has published three collections of poetry: *Carolina Cuban, Equivocaciones,* and *Bilingual Blues*.

Pérez-Firmat's work explores the pull between cultural identities. He often uses the tension between languages to depict the greater conflict. He uses linguistic puns and even "Spanglish" to create a humorous scenario for the contrast of cultures. His voice is one of someone who is trying to come to terms with a double identity. Pérez-Firmat is known for his provocative essays on Miami and has a new collection of essays on growing up in Miami titled *Next Year in Cuba,* from which we have included two excerpts.

THREE MAMBOS AND A MONTUNO

Mambo #3: *The House of Mirrors*

One of the landmarks of Cuban Miami is a restaurant called Versailles, which has been located on Eighth Street and Thirty-Fifth Avenue for many years. About the only thing this Versailles shares with its French namesake is that it has lots of mirrors on its walls. One goes to the Versailles not only to be seen, but to be multiplied. This quaint, kitschy, noisy restaurant that serves basic Cuban food is a paradise for the self-absorbed: the Nirvana of Little Havana. Because of the bright lights, even the windows reflect. The Versailles is a Cuban panoptikon: you can lunch, but you can't hide. Who goes there wants to be the stuff of visions. Who goes there wants to make a spectacle of himself (or herself). All the *ajiaco* you can eat plus all the jewelry you can wear multiplied by the number of reflecting planes — and to top it off a waitress who calls you *mi vida*.

Across the street at La Carreta, another popular restaurant, the food is the same (both establishments are owned by the same man) but the feel is different. Instead of mirrors La Carreta has booths. There you can ensconce yourself in a booth and not be faced with multiple images of yourself. But at the Versailles there is no choice but to bask in self-reflective glory.

For years I have harbored the fantasy that those mirrors retain the blurred image of everyone who has paraded before them. I think the mirrors have a memory, as when one turns off the TV and the shadowy figures remain on the screen. Every Cuban who has lived or set foot in Miami over the last three decades has, at one time or another, seen himself or herself reflected on those shiny surfaces. It's no coincidence that the Versailles sits only two blocks away from the Woodlawn Cemetery, which contains the remains of many Cuban notables, including Desi Arnaz's father, whose remains occupy a niche right above Gerardo Machado's. Has anybody ever counted the number of Cubans who have *died* in Miami? Miami is a Cuban city not only because of the number of Cubans who live there but also because of the number who have died there.

The Versailles is a glistening mausoleum. The history of Little Havana — tragic, comic, tragi-comic — is written on those spectacular specular walls. This may have been why, when the mirrors came down in 1991, there was such an uproar that some of them had to be put back. The hall of mirrors is also a house of spirits. When the time comes for me to consume my last tropical soup, I intend to disappear into one of the mirrors (I would prefer the one on the right, just above the expresso machine). My idea of immortality is to become a mirror image at the Versailles.

Montuno: Banana Boats and Havana Beats

Back in the mid-eighties there was a popular Latin discotheque in Miami called The Banana Boat. "El platanito de Kendall," as it was sometimes called, featured live music by many of the exponents of the so-called Miami Sound. One night I was there to hear Willie Chirino, a popular Cuban-American singer who is something like the Billy Joel of the YUCAS. In addition to going through his repertoire of hits, Chirino played a traditional *son montuno* by Miguel Matamoros called "El son de la loma." Now this song is really an inquiry into the essence of *cubanía,* an inquiry that takes the form of a question about the birthplace of the members of the Mátamoros trio. In the opening lines a young girl asks her mother where the singers, *los cantantes,* come from: "Mamá yo quiero saber, de donde son los cantantes." The punning answer is that the singers hail from the hills but sing on the plain, "son de la loma y cantan en llano." "Llano" means both "plain" and a way of singing and "son" means both "they are" and the name of the music in which the reply is framed.

One of the people in the audience that night was José Fajardo, a gifted flutist who in the fifties led Fajardo y Sus Estrellas, a Cuban *charanga* second only to the Orquesta Aragón in quality and acclaim. When Chirino began to play, Fajardo went up on the stage, took out his wooden flute, and — *sin estrellas pero brillante* — joined in the *son*. What then followed was a *montuno* memorable for the extended counterpoint between Chirino's American keyboard and Fajardo's Cuban flute. Given that this musical mix was taking place only a few blocks from a strip mall called Loehman's Plaza, in my mind the "Son de la loma" became the "Song of Loehman's," and as such a moving, melodious emblem of the acts of translation that make up Cuban-American culture. Acts of translation: *loma* and Loehmann's; *son* and song; Havana beats and Banana Boats. It was remarkable enough to hear the "Son de la loma" in a Banana Boat; but to hear it played in tandem by Chirino and Fajardo seemed little short of marvelous.

That night I realized where the *son* went when it left Cuba: to Kendall.

RICARDO PAU-LLOSA

*R*icardo Pau-Llosa (1954–   ) is a poet and art critic. He was born in Havana and has lived in Florida since 1960. Currently, he is a professor in the English Department at Miami-Dade Community College, Kendall Campus, where he teaches creative writing and composition.

As an art critic, Pau-Llosa has been important in promoting modern Latin American art throughout the hemisphere and Europe. He has curated numerous exhibits worldwide and authored several art books and catalogs. His art criticism has appeared in numerous magazines, among them *Arts, Arts Papers, Connaissance des Arts*, and *Interview*. He regularly lectures on art history as well.

Pau-Llosa has also played a significant role as a poet. He is probably the Cuban-American poet of his generation who has received the most exposure and recognition in the United States, his work appearing in almost every literary magazine in the U.S. He has come full circle in exploring his Cuban cultural identity, from his first book, *Sorting Metaphors*, where he uses mythological and intellectual metaphors to deal with his angst, to *Cuba*, a direct exploration of his roots through a predominantly narrative style.

Sorting Metaphors won the national competition for the first Anhinga Poetry Prize, judged in 1983 by William Stafford. Pau-Llosa's second book of poems, *Bread of the Imagined*, was published by Bilingual Press (1992), and his last book, *Cuba*, was published by Carnegie Mellon University Press (1993).

FRUTAS

*G*rowing up in Miami any tropical fruit I ate
could only be a bad copy of the Real Fruit of Cuba.
Exile meant having to consume false food,
and knowing it in advance. With joy
my parents and grandmother would encounter
Florida-grown mameyes and caimitos at the market.
At home they would take them out of the American bag
and describe the taste that I and my older sister
would, in a few seconds, be privileged to experience
for the first time. We all sat around the table
to welcome into our lives this football-shaped,
brown fruit with the salmon-colored flesh
encircling an ebony seed. "Mamey,"
my grandmother would say with a confirming nod,
as if repatriating a lost and ruined name.
Then she bent over the plate,
slipped a large slice of mamey into her mouth,
then straightened in her chair and, eyes shut,
lost herself in comparison and memory.
I waited for her face to return with a judgment.
"No, not even the shadow of the ones back home."
She kept eating, more calmly,
and I began tasting the sweet and creamy pulp
trying to raise the volume of its flavor
so that it might become a Cuban mamey. "The good
Cuban mameyes didn't have primaveras," she said
after the second large gulp, knocking her spoon
against a lump in the fruit and winking.
So at once I erased the lumps in my mental mamey.
I asked her how the word for "spring"
came to signify "lump" in a mamey. She shrugged.
"Next you'll want to know how we lost a country."

ASSIMILATION

*T*he round man who owns the restaurant
rises from his table of red pasta and thin blondes
pulling one up with him to dance.
Behind a stiff smile she feels like wreckage
sucked in by a doomed liner.
He tangos her to a Neapolitan song
immigrants used to sing.
She is profoundly blonde and cannot read
the clumsy joy in his Vesuvian face
or the two karat tear his lashes swallow.
A tambourine crooner deafens us: "So long
as there is sun, so long as there is sea,
a girl next to one's heart, a song to sing.
Who has given has given, who has received
has received. Let's forget the past,
we are all from Napoli, paisan."

I am from Cuba, Chagito,
and I have grown round with patience.
I bear what passes for a pig-headed heart.
My colleagues in America have contributed
to the swelling of my cheeks
each time I say No to their tyrant of choice.
So I am stuck in love with a place I do not know.
My immigrations consist of drifting in place
and impregnating American air with my cigar.
I know how to echo the rhythms
of mercy's blondes that float my way.
I am no gourmet but I've trained
my loss like a dog to guard stupidly a destiny.

The Napoli dance is briefly over.
He returns the first girl to his table
and pulls up a fresh one who clings to him
as seaweed to an aimless hull
even as he cartwheels her by the waist
again and again.
We are near that sea that sings away
the distance to Cuba only
if you have dreamt her long and hard,
with no choice in the matter,
perfectly still, quiet, and broken.

LA HISTORIA ME ABSOLVERA

After the painting "The Swimmer"
by Paul Sierra

*I*nto a gold leaf light odds are
a man thrown from a raft
will raise his head and take no solace
from being one with the horizon
or from not being, which will be soon now
with the next leaden wave, the fist
of a world not his own and into which he fled
hoping simply to cross it,
but as it turned out
he slipped into God's belly
and no bells sang, no sign said
this is cowardice or honor,
fear or martyrdom,
no Lord would make him, one day, come out

from the cavernous water or have his angels clap
as the man tumbles out of leviathan and onto the sand
to shoulder destinies, because this man
tried to leave paradise, and only one in four make it,
and he was swallowed by history,
while somewhere a future is being plotted
like tides from a satellite,
a tyrant is being called necessity
and a death is being
called nothing at all.

DOS RIOS

*M*anhattan, Central Park South, falling
beneath first snow from a bronze
horse three times life, you are dwarfed
by New York. In truth, you wrote about just
one subject: freedom and its monsters.
You went to your death on your first charge
shot from a bronze horse somewhere
between me, November and a few pigeons.

Martí, the bums are watching. Maybe not.
Some of them will finally join the group
of exiles already entranced by your oratory.
A second war, a last war, Patria
seemed less dangerous a word.
After all, this was the nineteenth century
and though you may not have sounded like it,
you must have looked the stiff professor, right
hand pointing in the air, proper if humble suit,
coat over your left wrist. They want action,
not words. You fight, we'll follow.

Playitas, Oriente Province, 1895.
The landing and soon death.
Everyday your words become the flesh
that a nation devours. For a long time
only the bones have been left,
but they will do in famine's hour,
bones like white roses,
passions like bones like white roses.
Yours is, after all, the only century of patrias.
I must choose, mustn't I, what century to live in
unless, like you, the choices have been made
and one simply finds them in the snow,
between the rivers.

ROBERTO FERNANDEZ

R oberto Fernández (1952–) was born in Sagua la Grande and has lived in Florida since 1961. He spent his teenage years in Palm Beach, where his parents still live. He has spent most of his adult life in Tallahassee, where he lives with his own family and teaches at Florida State University.

Fernández, a novelist, was the first to satirize Miami's Cuban community in English in his novel *Raining Backwards*. He also published *La vida es un Special* and *La montaña rusa* in the early 1980s. He is currently working on a new novel, *Holy Radishes*, which deals with, as he says, "the contact between rednecks and the dethroned Cuban burgeoisie" around the Clewiston central Florida sugar area. "Fairview" included here is an excerpt from that novel.

Fernández has won several awards, including a Fellowship from the Florida Arts Council in 1993.

FAIRVIEW

$\mathcal{M}$rs. James B. opened the cans of beans and weenies and corn niblets and then dipped three spoons of lard in the heated skillet. As the lard began to melt, she placed the biscuits in the oven and stirred the gravy. When the melted lard started crackling, she covered her face with a rag and submerged the chicken quarters in the scalding bubble bath. She always covered her face to prevent stray drops of liquid lard from marring her face.

When she finished cooking, realizing her face was still swollen, she applied an ice packet to the area under the eye. She held the ice against her cheek for a few minutes while she munched on a drumstick with her free hand, sucking the marrow with gusto. When the ice cubes disappeared, she placed the food in the oven, then walked to her bedroom, licking her lips on the way. Mrs. James B. opened the second left drawer of her dresser and looked for her makeup kit. Her swollen cheek was red and cold when she applied the bronze color base to cover the bluish marks under her eye. She wet her lips, using them as a palette to dip her index finger and get rid of the excess makeup. She changed out of her jeans and blouse and put on a house dress, preparing for her husband's return.

Mrs. James B. paced up and down the house as she waited. To ease her fear, she tried to remember her day as Miss Technical Mark. She had appeared clad in an itsy-bitsy red bikini on top of a washing machine, saying with a big smile while she raised her left leg towards her shoulder and winked her right eye, "Ingenious innovations in household appliances mean more free time for love."

The telephone rang and Mrs. James B. rushed to answer.

"Hello."

"I ain't coming home til late."

"Why? Something come up with the baseball team?"

"I said I'm gonna be late. I gotta meeting."

"Then it must be something having to do with sports."

"Don't be so nosy, woman. It ain't got nothing to do with sports. But don't let my supper get cold!"

"But . . ."

Click.

Mrs James B. sighed in relief.

The Captain of the Leon High School football squad usually arrived with a big commotion, burning rubber, honking the horn of his wild Mustang, and cursing his luck. He would slam the screen door and go straight for the ice box, searching for his brew. He could drink a can in a single gulp, crush it with his fist, then throw it against the kitchen wall to signal Mrs. James B. he was ready to eat. Sometimes he would skip dinner and put down a six-pack, slip into his old football jersey, and play with an invisible ball. Mrs. James B.'s job was to stand by his side and cheer him on to make the winning touchdown. Then he would suddenly stop his final play and shout he was still the most valuable player that sorry squad ever had, that he had more balls than anyone else in the history of Leon High School. Then he would complain she wasn't cheering loud enough and that it was her fault he had hurt his knee and he didn't make the last cut with the Chicago Bears.

"You told me I was getting fat so I ran as fast as I could and I tripped against one of the hurdles, and it's your fucking fault, you bitch!" he would shout in anger.

Sometimes Mrs. James B. would forget the very first time he beat her up, the day he punctured her womb, and remind him that she had nothing to do with his knee injury and that he didn't make the final selection because Craig Moody made the impressive throw which convinced the coaches to draft him instead. Then all hell would break loose and he would chase her around the living room, tackle her, and beat her up once more, calling her a goddamn liar. Later in the evening, a contrite captain would kiss her and beg her forgiveness.

Though this evening it was going to be different. He wasn't coming until late. Mrs. James B. pushed a chest of drawers to one side and reached behind it, looking for the old photo album she had constructed from the Pawn Shop pictures. It had a mother of pearl cover. She opened it up to the page she had marked with a peice of toilet paper and where she had pasted the last three pictures she had bought. She had convinced Stanley to give her one extra picture for all her previous purchases. Fifty-seven black-and-white pictures depicted her family history. Two recent snapshots of a boy and a girl graced a new page. She had inscribed on the back: "To Mom, I'm playing some mean football this year. The academy stinks. I can't wait to eat your biscuits and gravy. Love you, your son James B. IV." For the second picture she used pink ink and dotted every "i" with a small black-eyed-susan. "Mommy, Seth asked me to go steady with him. His father is the wealthiest man in Oglethorpe County. I am wearing my favorite dress so you can see it in the picture. I love you, your daughter, Missy."

"Nellie ain't goin' to outdo me," she said as she closed the album and headed for Nellie's place.

Nellie was surprised to see Mrs. James B. striding across her yard and to hear the rapid thudding of her shoes as she came up the five steps to her porch. Mr. James B. must be away on a game. Nellie rushed to the door and before Mrs. James B. had a chance to yell her traditional "yoohoo," the door opened.

"Mrs. James B., what a pleasant surprise! Don't tell me there is an early shipment at the packing house!"

"I hope I ain't interrupting anything."

"Oh, no. Nelson is working overtime and the children are playing outside," Nellie reassured her friend.

"I just had to come over. Mama finally sent me our family album and I had to show you. She took her sweet time. These are mostly pictures of Fairview, the family plantation. You must be careful not to touch them. These were the ones the Yankees didn't get."

"Oh, Mrs. James B," Nellie said in shock. "Did another bee get you? That side of your face is swollen."

"It wasn't a bee this time. This time a wasp zapped me. They're building a nest by my back door. I went out to the clothesline and on my way back that nasty little son-of-gun got me."

"I will go and get you some Chinese balm. It will make it go down in a few minutes. It's made from powdered truffles. You just make yourself comfortable while I get you the balm."

Mrs. James B. sat down on the couch rehearsing in her mind the narrative of her family history, especially the parts she thought would impress Nellie the most.

"Here you are. A small quantity will make it go away." Nellie dabbed her finger in the small container and spread it over the swollen area.

"Thanks, Nel," Mrs. James B. said with feeling, which took Nellie aback. "This is the album, Nellie. You be careful when you turn the pages. It's very old, not as old as that city in Mexico I told you about a while back but old enough."

Smelling of tiger balm, Mrs. James B. began her family saga.

"Be careful, Nellie! Lick your finger. It's easier that way. That's Fairview. It had beautiful French windows, a real Frenchman from France put them up. The flowers tumbling over the verandas are wisteria. There ain't none in this area, but in Fairview they grew as wild as weeds. The trees lining the driveway were cedars and my great-great-grandfather had the slaves plant them. The Yankees chopped them down to keep warm in the winter and left none for us when they knew we were hungry and just barely alive! Flip the page, Nellie. This is my great-grandmother; her name was Amanda Bailey. She was the tallest woman in the county. Look at her beautiful inky lashes. I wish I had got them, but my sister beat me to it. I got these droopy ones from my father's side of the family. Those ain't relatives. Those are the Negro servants. Probably relatives of Naomi, the colored woman that works with us in the packing house. That's why I don't talk to her. I'm sure her relatives helped the Yankees destroy Fairview. Amanda was an expert dealing with her Negroes. She told them what to do once and didn't let them get sassy with her. That's my great-grandfather. Amanda's husband; his name was Red."

"Are you related to Red Hotel from the fish market?" Nellie asked.

"Well, Nellie Mae, we ain't white trash. It's a nickname because his hair is red. Red wasn't that cute. He had sort of a funny nose, like a carrot, but he was as shrewd as a weasel. He could sell you just about anything he wanted."

"Who are the twins?"

"Them two little girls on his lap are my granny and her sister Sarah. They dressed in the best French fabrics money could buy. The French make a lot of things like windows and doors and fries."

"My father always got our lace from Belgium, from his friend Christian," Nellie added proudly.

"Well, now that I think about it, one of the twins dressed in Belgium fabrics and fine stuff like that."

"And the horse?"

"That fireball belonged to Granny. She rode it every morning and almost fell from it while jumping a hurdle. I'm sure glad she didn't because if she had, yours truly wouldn't be talking to you right now. Not so fast, Nellie. I took my time when you showed me yours."

"Excuse me. I'm developing poor manners. What's that?"

"That's the barbecue. It was one of the few things the dawn Yankees left standing. I reckon they couldn't burn a place that's used for burning. Flip that page right quick!"

"What is it, Mrs. James B.?"

Mrs. James B. started an uncontrollable sobbing and Nellie did her best to calm her down.

"It's the picture of my great-aunt Sarah as a grown woman. She was shot by a Yankee soldier. She had a hearing problem and when the soldier shouted

'Freeze,' she didn't hear him and she got it right in her forehead."

"I understand, Mrs. James B. Believe me, I understand your suffering, your humiliation. Don't you worry, I can assure you, you will be with me at Mondovi."

"She was engaged to be married. Her beau called her
'Sweetheart.' Ain't that sweet?

"That's my great-grandma and Granny. They worked as nurses during the war. My great-grandma shot two Yankees that were abusing her favorite Negro servant; so much for their equality crap. Then great-Granny lost her mind. She thought my grandma's pet rabbit was her husband and prepared what little was there to eat for him. There were days my grandma told me she had to watch the rabbit eat her share. Then great-Granny started having headaches and throwing up and she believed herself to be pregnant by the rabbit. Grandma was so hungry in the Winter of '65 she took the rabbit, strung him by the neck, made a fire and had it for supper all by herself. Flip that page before I start crying again.

"That's Granny in the hospital when she got gangrene and the doctor cut her middle finger. Oh, Nellie, look! That's my great-grand and her dress. She made it out of a curtain. That's so sad, so sad. When Fairview was sacked the first time, General Sherman stole all of my great-grand's party dresses to take north to his ugly wife."

"Just like what happened to me. It wasn't a general but a fat commander, though he wasn't a commander then. I can't bear to say his name. He stole all my dresses for his mistresses."

"Did he really?"

"Yes, but I don't wish to discuss it."

"Whatever suits you, honey. That's our hometown before that shit-head General set it afire. That was on a Wednesday, and the following day they rode to Fairview and burned it to the ground, stole all our family jewels, even my great-great-grandfather's sword. He fought against you people in Mexico. That's how he got that sword. They were so nasty, those damn soldiers, they threatened to cut off Granny's finger if she didn't give the General her gold thimbles."

"Did she?"

"Let's just say she kept her finger. That one is the last picture of baby Audry. The only picture left. Her mother was a friend of my great-grand. I think her name was Beverly Norton, but everybody called her Lee because she looked so much like General Lee. Anyway, Lee gave birth three months before the town fell. Baby Audry was stolen by a union soldier whose wife was barren and taken up north." Mrs. James B. began to cry with loud wails.

"Calm down, Mrs. James B. Calm down. I'll make you some coffee."

"I'll be OK, Nellie. Just open that window. I need some fresh air. Forget about the coffee."

"Cry more if you have to. I know how painful memories can create havoc in your mind."

Mrs. James B. took a wiff of fresh air and pretended to calm down.

"What about that trip to Mondovi, Nellie? Do you have a big house there with a hairy swarthy man like that picture you showed me?"

"It's not a house, it's a palazzo and our friend Sergio is much nicer looking than the swarthy man. Sergio has the beauty of something unattainable . . . his eyes are two still lakes in which your soul can attain tranquility. He will take you by the hand and personally escort you throughout the city. He will introduce you to the best of society and tell them about your family's humiliation and misfortune. They will all understand your years of suffering in silence, and in a few days, you will be the talk of Mondovi. But, Mrs. James B., you must not tell anyone about this trip. Not even Mr. James B."

"I cross my heart and swear to die. I won't tell a soul."

CARLOS VICTORIA

*C*arlos Victoria (1950–) was born in Camaguey. He began writing at a young age and in 1965 won a short-story contest sponsored by the magazine *El Caimán Barbudo*. For political reasons, in 1971, he was expelled from the University of Havana where he was studying English literature. Following his expulsion, he worked nine years as a laborer in the Forestry Department in his province. Finally, in 1980, he left Cuba through the port of Mariel, becoming one of numerous writers in exile known as the "Mariel Writers." Since then, his short stories have been published in many magazines and anthologies in the United States and France. In 1985, one of his stories appeared in the annual issue of *Le Monde*.

His first novel, *La travesía secreta*, was a finalist in the 1991 Letras de Oro literary contest. In 1992, he published the collection of stories *Las sombras en la playa* (Shadows on the Beach), which contains the story we have included here. Recently, his novel *Puente en la oscuridad* won the first place in the Letras de Oro literary contest. Victoria calls it a novel "of existential terror."

The author lives in Miami where he also works for *The Miami Herald*.

SHADOWS ON THE BEACH

to Luis de la Paz

*B*ecause that August day was hot and humid, and the crowds filled the beaches, darkening the sand and the water with their myriad races, Cesar continued up Collins Avenue up to Haulover Beach where he thought he might find a more peaceful spot. Although he always preferred peace and quiet, and avoided the crowds and the noise, on this occasion he had another reason to look for a place where he could be alone: his elderly mother was with him, and she too shared with her son this secret aversion to tumultuousness.

Was it fear, timidity, or some mysterious kind of selfishness? Given the singular nature of his mother and him, it became difficult to specify the answer. In the mother, love for others had dissolved itself in the sterility brought on by realizing the truth; as for the son, perhaps because of this very failure, there had developed a kind of strange intensity in regard to others that, although he feigned it at all costs, remained latent even when dealing with people who were strangers to him; this hidden vehemence risked the uncertain harmony of his very movements.

From one end to the other, Haulover's long strip of sand offered its show of bodies. But after walking awhile, the awkward couple settled for an open space next to a rundown lifeguard stand. Under the shadow of this shack, the mother laid down the towels and carefully placed the cooler with the soft drinks, as if she were setting a table for a Christmas dinner, or making the bed where some important guest would spend the night.

This was always her way of doing things. But in reality, family dinners were already a thing of the distant past, of the days of her youth in Cuba, and only her son had slept under the same roof as she during all these years. She then sat down, not without difficulty, onto the plush towels, totally dressed, as if instead of being at the beach she were resting on a park bench, and she ran her curious gaze over the surroundings, satisfied to see that the bathers were off at a certain distance. Cesar, mocking his mother's unwillingness to don her bathing suit, ran to the shore.

That instant of entering the water produced an unspeakable pleasure, and now in Guanabo the raucous crowd of students imparted the waves with a certain warm rhythm. His school friends surrounded him flailing their arms, and in an instant he saw himself dragged by several pairs of hands toward the deep end, where he could not reach bottom with his feet, for they all knew that he had not yet learned to swim and took pleasure in frightening him. He struggled to free himself from those hands, and finally let himself be taken in the midst of coughs and laughter, as the salt burned in his mouth.

But Guanabo was already a worn name, a mere fallen leaf, and the hands that grabbed his body had been absent as if obedient to a silent agreement: today it would not be necessary to fight to unclench them. Besides, with time Cesar had become an able swimmer, even if not an outstanding one, the same as had happened in every other aspect of his life. He swam a few strokes over the wavetops and then waved with his hand at the old woman who watched him protected from the sun by the shadow of the lifeguard stand.

In one of the photographs that she kept from her days as a young teacher, his mother lay on the sand next to a beautiful girl; in front of them a corpulent man stared at them intently with the insistence of a frozen image, like that which we try in vain to duplicate in real life. On the back of the picture with careful lettering was written the place: *La Concha Beach, Havana.* And underneath the date: *1948.*

But when Cesar visited *La Concha,* it was already known as *Braulio Coroneaux,* the new name which the revolutionary government had assigned to it in its unbridled zeal to change things. This beach also brought Cesar a dark memory: in it, he had seen some men pull from the sea a drowned body. It was October and the beach was deserted; Nora, shaking her hair, asked him not to look. But a noxious curiosity made him look at the bluish deformed face of that ageless body, whose anguished expression later reappeared in Cesar's dreams.

"Let's leave this place," said Nora. "Drowned people are bad luck."

To Nora everything was a matter of good or bad luck: she was naive and superstitious, and her nipples stood out through her almost transparent blouse. That afternoon they said goodbye to their bad mood in front of the old Coney Island; Cesar coldly kissed her on the cheek when the bus arrived.

But the unknown dead are different from those one has seen alive, and Cesar remembered as he swam that Ernesto had ceased to exist two months ago when he was coming back on the Palmetto Expressway after a night of alcohol and marijuana: the steering wheel had sunk into his chest as a result of the crash.

Every time Cesar floated on the waves his mind would wander to the thought of death, though this neither scared him nor made him anxious, but rather made him feel pleasantly sleepy.

He fell on the sand next to his mother who, as she rubbed lotion on his back, quietly said to him:

"That man looks like him."

Him; in the elaborate language between mother and son over some thirty years, composed of a capricious terminology at times not entirely exempt of good humor, meant Cesar's father who had abandoned both of them when the mother had given birth. The passage of time had made it so that mentioning *him* was not painful, but rather inadequate, as in a vulgar expression in a courteous conversation between two people who barely know each other.

From the other side of the stand, a fiftyish man with greying hair and a protruding chin covered with sand the body of a child, probably his son, enjoying the task as if he too were a kid.

"In what is he like him?" asked Cesar, who, although he had never known his father, had seen photographs from the early days of courting, and now found nothing familiar in the weathered features of that man.

"I don't know," answered the mother. "But he has a certain air, especially in the nose and the mouth."

"Now, don't get sentimental," said Cesar smiling, and he decided to go back to the water so as to avoid a dangerous conversation. Yet, as he went by the man, he peered at him indiscreetly, and he thought that his mother was right: there was something of his father's features in that face. At that moment, the stranger said in a loud voice, in Spanish with a Cuban accent:

"One time in Varadero Beach I overslept under the sun one whole afternoon, and they had to take me to the hospital with sunstroke. I spent about a month molting."

"You were probably drunk," said the boy with a laugh.

"How dare you call your father a drunkard," said the man, and he threw a fistful of sand on the boy's face. "Is this how you show respect for your father?"

The boy got out from the sandhole with some difficulty and both started horsing around as they yelled and laughed. Cesar walked away slowly without looking away, and for awhile he was not able to forget the metallic sound of the old man's voice.

Now in the surf, a disquieting question occurred to him: What must his father's voice have been like? In the last few months, he had been obsessed by two voices, both of which he could listen to thanks to the magic of recording. One was the voice of a friend in a cassette tape sent to him from Spain, a voice whose singular timbre Cesar had not heard in ten years. This friend had played a crucial role in his youth. To recognize his voice on the tape recorder, this dear but almost forgotten voice, made him remember the nights when they would talk in the attic of the building where they both lived, and this scene appeared to him with such clarity that for many hours it seemed to him that by opening the window he would see Havana with its jumble of lights and shadows, framed by the darkness of the sea.

The other voice, the one which belonged to an unknown face, was that of the husband of the woman with whom he was currently in love. The man remained in Cuba waiting, like so many others, to leave for the exile community, and he would send her tape recordings in which he would reaffirm his hope. Cesar had refused to listen to it at first, for he feared being jealous at the sound of that voice, but later, after listening to the serene words, he discovered that the important things for those one loves — and he had indeed grown to love this woman — should not cause any torment or bitterness. And now, to this sequence of confusing thoughts a new uncertainty was added: the voice of his unknown father.

On the very shore, the group of friends tried to open beer bottles with their teeth; the cabanas of Santa Lucia shimmered under the afternoon sun. When Cesar emerged gasping from the water after a long dive, he found Jorge spitting blood on the sand, his gums bruised by the sharp bottle caps.

"It serves you right for being stupid," said Cesar, emptying a beer bottle all over his hair.

"It's obvious you didn't pay for it," shouted Tito, and immediately a whirlpool of dust broke loose on the hillside, as if advising the vacationers that the season was over. All summers in Santa Lucia ended that way, with the wind in the trees and empty beer bottles, and a bit of a taste of blood on one's lips.

But now the kid had jumped on the old man's back: one could not hear what they were shouting about. Seeing the man horsing around with his son made Cesar remember that one time he had come to Haulover with a friend from work. The amiable and lively young man brought with him an inflatable raft, and while wrestling in the water to see who could end up with the raft out in the deep end, the young man suddenly kissed him on the neck. Cesar gave him a surprised look, as he did not suspect that his friend harbored such inclinations. But the expression on his friend's face led him to think that perhaps it was a joke. Then, with long strokes, they slipped through the water along the length of the pier. A nude sunbather enjoyed herself with her lover next to a rusty old boat, seemingly adrift, with paused rhythmic motions: the boat, the couple.

Yes, thought Cesar, eroticism disconcerted him. It had been his fate to do battle against an able fighter, against a sneaky rival. During his last alcoholic crisis, which lasted more than three months, Cesar walked into a seedy bar one night wasted to a total blur; women were taking their clothes off on a stage next to the bar, and one of them, somewhat buxom but with an attractive face, combed her pubic hairs with the heel of her shoe while the jukebox played one of Fleetwood Mac's latest hits. That figure on the stage, with its sinuous movements and the evocative background music, excited him to a state of exasperation, and he left the place immediately, feeling feverish, inadequate, and with the vague intention of humiliating someone's body; he ended up in the arms of a prostitute who stole his money and left him unconscious in a hole of a room in some sordid motel.

In the water, the simulated fight between father and son had come to an end, and while he devoured some slices of cold fried chicken, Cesar suddenly felt the desire to speak to the old man. But the thought that this might upset his mother, who was sensitive and fickle, made him forget the idea. He then lounged back on the towel to catch some sun. Next to the sea the hours flew by rapidly, he thought; they were not at all like the others, those of work or sleeplessness, or of the simple act of waiting for that which never comes.

With the afternoon's heat in his face, he did not realize when Caridad had sat down beside him; when he felt her hand on his mouth, all he could do was to bite her fine fingers, on which a ring recalled an old promise once hurriedly made beneath a leafless tree. In that instant, she lay down on top of him, squeezing her breasts against his face, suffocating him. Night fell on the fishing port. The strumming of a guitar could be heard behind the marsh and the mangroves.

Now his mother said:

"He doesn't look that much like him."

"What?" asked Cesar, who in his drowsiness did not understand the words.

"I said that man doesn't look that much like him."

Cesar once again glanced at the stranger, thinking that most times love makes for resemblance: despite so many years gone by, his mother had never forgotten the one man she had loved. But her face revealed a gentle smile and Cesar ventured a joke:

"If it were him I don't think you would still like him."

"I'm too old to be thinking about such things," said the mother laughing, and she stuck her head through the porthole window to look at the multitude of boats anchored in the port, waiting for permission to leave. The waters of Mariel Bay violently buffeted the ship, making it sway in a nauseating manner. The emigrants' bodies squeezed in on themselves, lethargic after nights of waiting, shameless in their exhaustion.

Glancing at the stranger, Cesar remembered that when he had turned eighteen years old, he had decided to visit his father, and found out his address through a distant relative. The Santo Suarez area of the city was not familiar to him: with hesitant steps he walked up Juan Delgado street. The roots of the trees had destroyed the sidewalks, cracking the cement with their deformed contours, covered with dark moss. The facades of buildings protected their interiors like a wall protects a fort. In the silence of noon, his steps resounded with a sinister echo.

Years later, sitting across from a friend in a Miami restaurant, he confessed that upon arriving at his father's house he did not knock on the door.

"I'm glad you didn't do it," said the friend, and the sincere sound of his words moved Cesar, for it was the first time that he ever spoke of this and he did not regret that he had chosen as a confidant the young man who with his hands upon the table gazed at him sympathetically. His friend's hands were white and shapely, and listening to him Cesar felt like reaching out with his own hands to touch his friend's in gratitude. But at that very point where two people meet after a long journey, gestures become unnecessary: perhaps to nod with one's head is enough.

With the afternoon waning, the sea became magnified. The waves rose like thick walls and the refugee–filled boats ran the risk of sinking in the Florida Straits. The waters by the shore are different; near them, the father plays with the son, and the mother dozes off in the shade of the old lifeguard stand.

Presently the father knows that now this day with his most beloved son has come to an end. Night creeps up along the red horizon sprinkled with the flight of migrating birds. His voice when calling the boy conveys impatience, though tenderness at the same time, and the mother carefully folds the beach towels while Cesar enters the water for the last time.

At Santa Cruz del Sur Beach, he is one of the few who swim at this hour; by the pier, one can still see the debris left there in the wake of the hurricane of '32. But now only a few fishermen can remember the event; the jumble of timbers and algae seem to Cesar to be more the result of neglect than of a catastrophe.

With his hair dripping water, Cesar now approached the dressed figure by the lifeguard stand, and he was not surprised that his mother's lips moved while her eyes remained fixed on the sand. It was easy for him to guess that in this instant she was not muttering just some soliloquy, nor a prayer learned by heart; beneath the setting afternoon sun, before the intensely green waters, his mother seemed to feel an unknown harmony, and was perhaps saying it to herself. Or she was expressing her amazement aloud. Or she was giving thanks.

Translated by Ramón Bayardo Rancaño.

CAROLINA HOSPITAL

Carolina Hospital (1957–) is a poet and prose writer residing in Miami, where she teaches writing and literature at Miami-Dade Community College. She was born in Havana. In 1961, her family left the island for Puerto Rico. Five years later, they moved to Miami, where she has lived ever since, except for seven years in Gainesville, Florida. There she attended the University of Florida and received degrees in English, Spanish, and Latin American studies, with an emphasis on migration.

Her own short fiction, essays, and poems have appeared in numerous national magazines and newspapers, including *The Washington Post, Prairie Schooner, Mid-American Review, Caribbean Writer, Vista, Rio Grande Review, Haydn Ferry Review, Appalachee Quarterly, Confrontation, Linden Lane,* and *Cuban Heritage Magazine.* She has also been included in numerous anthologies, among them *Looking For Home: Women Writing About Exile, Paper Dance: 55 Latino Poets, Barrios And Borderlands, Cool Salsa, Hispanic-Americans,* and *In Other Words: Literature By Latinas in the US.*

To date, she has published three books: *Cuban American Writers: Los Atrevidos; Everyone Will Have To Listen,* a bilingual edition of poetry by Tania Díaz Castro, translated by Hospital with Pablo Medina; and *The Instructor's Guide To Norton's New Worlds Of Literature,* co-authored with Carlos Medina.

She was the director of The Writer's Voice in Miami for two years and in 1994 was resident scholar for the Florida Center for Teachers of the Florida Humanities Council, leading the seminar "Los Latinos: U. S. and Florida."

HOW THE CUBANS
STOLE MIAMI

*T*he Cubans have stolen Miami.
("Will the last one to leave
bring the American flag?")
And from whom did we steal it?

From the Basque sailor who
gave Biscayne its name?
Or perhaps from the Spanish missionaries who lived
with the mosquitoes by the swampy bay?

In all fairness, we must admit
we stole it from the Tequesta or the Seminoles,
natives, driven north by
Andrew Jackson or south into the sea.

No, perhaps we stole it from the Spaniards
sent back to Havana after 300 years
of calling Florida home.
(And we complain about still being
in exile after only thirty-four.)

If we didn't steal it from the Indians or the Spaniards
it must have been the Conks,
Bahamians who built the railroads with hands of coal
while being told to be more Negro like their
neighbors to the north.

I know, we stole it from
Flagler, Tuttle, Merrick and Fisher
who catered to the rich but never to the Jewish.
(Only in Miami is a Jew an Anglo.)
If I see one more photo of Domino Park
I'll turn into a Jew.

Was it he, papi, who stole Miami?
He, who engineered from the Bacardi building to
One Biscayne Tower
and every school addition from Edison
to Homestead High?

No, it must have been my mother.
(What was it Joan Didion wrote,
"a mango with jewels?"
poor mother, so lean and trim.)
She spent 34 years volunteering
(Sacándole el kilo, my father would sneer.)

The Museum of Science,
Viscaya,
The Youth Center,
The Archdiocese,
Ballet Concerto,
La Liga Contra el Cancer,
The Mailman Center.
(A tour of Miami, you ask?)

Enough! says my dad,
locking up his checkbook tight.
"We're retiring out of Miami."
A new phenomenon,
"Cuban Flight,"
not to be confused with "White Flight."

If the Cubans have stolen Miami
and it's time they paid their dues,
then . . .

If I see one more photograph of Domino Park
who knows what I might do.

ON THE DEATH OF
ROBERTO VALERO

*W*hen I saw Francis wander the narrow streets
and dark alleys of Assisi, the other day,
I did not expect to find you,
barefoot like a beggar.

Then, I did not know of your questions
to this sacred mendicant,
nor that you would join him
in your wounds and your humility.

It's good to remember that we are divine,
you once said.

In your suffering,
you saw the face of Christ and
did not demand to be lowered from the cross.

I was a student when I met you.
You had just arrived from Cuba through Mariel,
after seeking asylum in the Peruvian embassy.
You were already a published writer then,
but to me you looked like a young boy,
tired and disoriented.
When we finally spoke,
you broke into a smile,
a smile that would become familiar to me,
and your eyes glistened with mischief.
Through the years, your letters came
in mysterious envelopes with enigmatic addresses.
At first, they were brief, later
numerous pages from your diary.
You studied, wrote, married, bore children, and

taught, all before you were forty,
all in a foreign landscape of cold nights
and greetings in English.

When your body turned finite,
You did not pray for a cure,
but for a vision.
You did not pray to be spared,
but to be spared of radiation and resentment.

We dreamed
you were taken from us,
not by the plagues
and pestilences of medieval Assisi,
but by one of our own afflictions.

I searched for you,
Roberto, my Roberto,
who coined the name Carloslina
for Carlos and me,
husband and wife,
instead of brother and sister,
as you once thought,
who listened when we needed you to,
who publicly pleaded for reconciliation,
who comforted Reinaldo in *his* dying days.
No, Roberto,
you are neither defeat nor loss.
With your AIDS,
you too walked the streets of Jerusalem and Assisi.
Memories do not pass away easily
and in your memories
you have given us another glance at God.

THE GARDENER

I sit on the crisp grass
and slowly pull the weeds
around the newly planted
Manila palms and purple heather.
The dirt sneaks
into the creases in my skin.
I avoid the sun rays dappling the ground.
A gray covers the skies.
I let the scent of the warm soil,
the humidity in the air,
the stillness before the summer shower
transport me north
to the mountain forest,
of rhododendrons and spruce pine,
south to la finca,
with its cafetales and sugarcane fields.
For an instant, I exist in three spaces.
Back in my garden, I look around.
I realize it doesn't matter.
The hibiscus and bougainvilleas
I have planted
are blooming.
In any soil,
they are the same,
as long as they grow
nourished and unfettered.

DIONISIO MARTINEZ

*D*ionisio Martínez (1956–   ) is a poet born in Havana and raised in Guines. In 1965, at nine years of age, he went into exile with his family. He lived in Spain for a year and then resided in California from 1966 to 1972. At that time, he moved to Tampa where he continues to live and teach in the Poets-in-the-Schools program.

He is the author of *History as a Second Language*, recipient of *The Journal Poetry Award*, and published by Ohio State University Press in 1992. He has also published *Dancing at the Chelsea* with State Street Press. His work appears in a number of recent and forthcoming anthologies, including *The Best American Poetry 1992*, *The Jazz Poetry Anthology*, *A Walk on the Wild Side*, *Currents from The Dancing River*, and *Paper Dance: 55 Latino Poets*.

In 1993, Martínez received the Emerging Artists Grant from the Arts Council of Hillsborough County, Florida, and a *Mid-American Review* James Wright Poetry Prize. He has also won the Whiting Writer's Award.

Martínez writes in both Spanish and English. His most recent book, *Bad Alchemy*, was published by Norton Press in 1995, and he has recently completed a new manuscript in Spanish entitled *"El ojo se despide de la mano."*

Currently, he is an affiliate writer at the University of Tampa.

DANCING AT THE CHELSEA

*I*t is no longer a question of balance and yet
we dance to keep from falling.

We dance because the rough
surface of the moon has carved a hole in the dark.

We dance on the beams of our unfinished houses.
We were dancing when our real houses

vanished and our lives became this.
We dance because this thin European found

a piano in the hall and dragged it
into his room, and we had to celebrate

the way he dragged it in by himself
and the way he hacked at the keys like mad.

We are still dancing, still celebrating.
We dance with the ghost of Sid

Vicious in the elevator.
We were dancing before the murder.

We were dancing in the lobby when we heard
something and we all

felt a sharp pain and we thought it was only
our tired and reluctant muscles giving

up on our bodies. Now
we dance for the limousine driver and his family,

we dance for the genius, for the man
with a hole in his head, for the one who has

lived here forever.
We dance for every song ever

written about these rooms.
We dance full of vertigo looking

down from any window above 23rd Street,
we let ourselves

go like scarves in a confused wind.
We will be dancing after the man with

the hole in his head has burned
perfect circles through the soles of his shoes.

We will dance on the broken bones
of our feet. We think

we can go on even as ghosts, as angels looking
down at the blessings of 23rd Street.

We climbed the stairs dancing
the night of the blackout when the elevator

stopped. This was long before the ghost.
We still dance when we climb

and descend the stairs. We still
use the stairs because we like the romance of it.

We've danced through every modern war.
We dance

each night after the last club has closed down
like a war no one knows how to end and all

that remains is a scratched record and someone
humming and the inevitable piano

and all the lost angels in the halls.
We will be dancing when the last

angel cuts his own wings off and tosses them
to the moon and jumps like another

blessing from any window above 23rd Street.
We dance in spite of gravity and the failure

of perpetual motion, in spite of the sleepless
angels of mathematics.

We dance the dance of those who speak
in tongues.

We dance like the shadows
of puppets in someone's clumsy hands. Sometimes

we dance with our own clumsy shadows.
We dance to keep from falling in love with

the lives of the strangers we
picked when the lights went out. Some

of us lit candles. Remember? But this
was after the fact. In the dark

we had changed partners and now
we found ourselves clinging to strange

new lives. We knew
that it would be like this from here on.
We would dance
and dance, hoping that through friction

or obsolescence or possibly even perfect
balance we would rid ourselves

of these lives. This, at least,
was the hope that kept us dancing.

The truth was something else. We knew
that we would change partners again

and again like bums trading stolen
goods by the light of the small fire they've

made in the aisle of an abandoned Pullman.

SILVIA CURBELO

*S*ilvia Curbelo (1955–) was born in Matanzas and left the island with her family in 1966, at age eleven. She lived with her parents in Mexico City and Miami for short periods of time, and the family later settled in Carroll, a small town in the heart of Iowa, where her father taught Spanish for five years at the local high school. In 1973, she moved to Tampa, Florida, where she attended the University of South Florida and began focusing on her writing. She married Tom Errico in 1978 and has one daughter, Adrian, born in 1990.

Silvia has been awarded poetry fellowships from the National Endowment for the Arts, the Florida Arts Council, and the Cintas Foundation. She is a recipient of an Atlantic Center for the Arts Cultural Exchange Fellowship for Poetry to Chateau de la Napoule, in France (selected by John Ashbery), and a 1995 "Escape to Create" Fellowship from the Seaside Institute. In 1992, she was co-winner of the James Wright Poetry Prize from *Mid-American Review*.

A collection of poems, *The Geography of Leaving*, won the 1990 Gerald Cable Chapbook Competition and was published by Silverfish Review Press in 1991. Her work has appeared in *Kenyon Review*, *Prairie Schooner*, *Yellow Silk*, *Indiana Review*, *Bloomsbury Review*, *Linden Lane*, *Tampa Review*, and many other publications. Her poems have been collected in more than a dozen anthologies, including *More Light: Father and Daughter Poems*, *Currents from the Dancing River*, *Paper Dance: 55 Latino Poets*, and *Isle of Flowers*.

WISH

*T*he difference between then and now
could be wind lifting this page.
The memory of that house rises
like a wave and the world floats up
through its reflection.
I'm walking through weeds and old lace,
the simple furniture of grief.
Metaphors are what remain intact,
what are endlessly returning.
Here is childhood's blue pond,
the apple of sleep. All morning
the light seemed to swallow
all the light. You were wearing
a blouse made entirely of tiny fish
set adrift on a flat blue surface
that resembled the sea.
It wanted to be the sea.
Water is an abstraction
until you hold it to your lips.
The way sometimes a kiss belies
its own intentions, a wolf
in wolves' clothing.
In another story an apple dreams
itself into a rose, a pond
retraces someone's shadow
from memory and imagines
any cloud reflected
on its surface is a wave.
Some dreams are both bread
and hunger. Faith is
cool water under the tongue.
This story is an island.
A girl closes her eyes,
simple as an apple,
takes the first bite
like she's never been kissed.

DREAMING HORSE

after the painting by Franz Marc

I could lie down in all that blue.
I'm watching shadows tell
their own story, a pasture
that sleeps through anything.
The voice is a meadow, the river
is a wing. I wanted
to be there so completely
I thought this poem was you asleep,
your quiet breathing.
So many words keeping track.
The heart is an odd museum.
Sadnesses display themselves
in corners, in rooms
as empty as this field.
The hand denies the face,
the past lingers.
I let my voice climb out
of my cold shoes. It talks
to air, it conjures
what it needs, a landscape
without blame, a room
the color of a whisper.
When I think about love crawling
through this world exhausted
with no place left to fall
I could run circles around
the word. I could say it
to anyone. Listen. Somebody
dreamed this.

FOR ALL THE GOODBYES

*I*n a room not unlike this one
someone is always leaving someone else.

Someone blows out a candle.
Someone has finished the wine.

The single glove laid open
on the windowsill tells only

half the story. Try to imagine
the hundred metaphors for flight,

for endings, a door finally closing
and what is left behind—

the robe with its torn lining,
a scarf, cufflinks, an old shoe.

A man's abandoned overcoat
brings to mind

train stations, suitcases,
footsteps vanishing down the hall.

There is no mistaking
the closet door left ajar,

the empty hangers
like the thin shoulders

of loss, of distance.
If you have loved

someone like that
you have imagined his hands

opening other doors, unbuttoning
his shirt in other rooms.

Even as the buttons fall away
there is no turning back.

A dropped shoe is an island.
A scarf will break your heart.

MARISELLA VEIGA

*M*arisella Veiga (1957–) is a poet and fiction writer. She was born in Havana and came to the United States with her family in 1960. She was raised in St. Paul, Minnesota, and Miami, Florida. Veiga received a B.A. in English from Macalester College, Minnesota, and an M.F.A. in creative writing from Bowling Green State University in Ohio.

She lived two years in Puerto Rico where she worked as a freelance journalist. From there, she went to the Dominican Republic and spent three months as an artist-in-residence writing poetry and fiction in Altos de Chavón. She returned to Miami to edit *Aboard Inflight Magazine.*

Lately, Veiga has concentrated on writing fiction. She was a fiction workshop participant in the University of Miami's Summer Institute for Caribbean Creative Writing and was awarded an Institute Scholarship. Veiga has also attended the Bread Loaf Writer's Conference in Middlebury, Vermont, as a contributor.

Her poetry, essays, and translations have been published in numerous magazines and newspapers. Recently, her fiction has appeared in *Iguana Dreams: New Latino Fiction* and in *Currents from the Dancing River: Contemporary Latino Writing.* She currently teaches English at Miami-Dade Community College's Homestead Campus.

THE MOSQUITO NET

One Saturday afternoon, my neighbor Jack and I stood under a zinc awning, pretending to be interested in buying something on display in the window of the old department store. We were seeking relief from the sun. The longer we lingered, the more entertaining the goods became.

I pointed to a mosquito net hanging in the center of the showcase. Had he ever slept under one? Yes. No, he would not recommend it. Too hot. Jack moved away to get a closer look at some black fold-up umbrellas.

While he browsed, I took another look at the mosquito net. Designed for a single bed, it hung from the ceiling in fishing line. Its edges fell in a perfect rectangle around the upper portion of a girl mannequin. She looked like a stern toddler stuck inside a playpen. When I mentioned this to Jack, he said she seemed a little dusty. He suggested a fan, explaining the benefits of owning one. Besides keeping me cool, it would blow the mosquitoes away when I slept. . . . He leaned against a wall while I went inside the dark store to ask about the price of the portable fans.

Monday afternoon I bought one. There was nothing special about it: a white plastic body, blue plastic blades, two velocities. I had seen similar models spinning and turning from side to side in the doorways or apartments in the nearby housing project. Jack went with me to carry the package. When we returned, he set it on the floor. Then he did something he had never done. He took one of my hands, held it for a moment, then let it go. I didn't see him that evening.

The next morning, the fan was out of the box. I was satisfied with the purchase. As I wiped the dust off its metal covering, I thought about how it was made to protect living creatures from its dangerous, spinning blades. The metal would rust quickly, since the sea is always a few blocks away on an island. I thought about more affluent others who had fans perched in two corners of every room. I doubted a single fan would be sufficient.

For a long time, the fan stayed in the bedroom where no one would see it. It kept the mosquitoes away while I slept. That was the only time it was on. Jack was polite enough to not inquire about the fan when he came over for conversation after dinner. Even on the hottest nights he did not ask about it. Whenever we visited in his house, two ceiling fans continually spun, making his living room quite airy and comfortable.

One day, some people from the United States who were vacationing on the island came to visit. We sat in my living room, the three of them slouched on the sofa. I sat near the open front door on a wicker chair. We looked out the windows, admired the vegetation. I said how I was, they said how they were. After an hour or so of chit-chat, one of the guests, predictably enough the guy from Miami, got tired of the heat inside the house and asked, "Don't you have a fan?"

I didn't answer right away. The other two sat up a little then, preparing themselves to defend what they had obviously lacked the courage to ask. Their eyebrows were up. They waited. It was shameful to allow them to continue to suffer.

"Yes, I do," I said calmly. I got up from the chair slowly, so the wicker would creak. Slowly, as if the movement was costing me an extraordinary amount of effort.

I brought the fan to the center of the living room and placed it on the floor, where it was admired. The fan blew away some of the heat, but only a little of my guests' exasperation.

From that day on I moved the fan from room to room. The kitchen became more comfortable to cook in, so I started using the broiler. A fan works faster than a hair dryer, though my hairstyle changed considerably after using it for this purpose. It took the dampness out of the hand-washed garments that hadn't completely dried overnight.

By comparison, a mosquito net was useless.

And when the rains began, signalling fall, the weather cooled. I had begun sleeping with a blanket in addition to a sheet. I no longer wanted the fan's breeze. Without it, however, I was faced with the mosquito problem. I realized the fan's limitations.

On a Saturday afternoon again, I made a purchase. I shook the yards of white netting out on the floor, found the cloth loops on its ends and strung them with gold ribbons. I was glad I had not bought the cheaper, pink net. Its mesh seemed too large for safety, even though the old clerk assured me she had slept without mishap under one like it her entire life.

When the mosquito net was up it looked a perfectly soft box, an airy incubator. Getting into bed would be like climbing into a dream. I lifted one side of it up, got in, tucked the section under the mattress and abandoned the remainder of the afternoon for a nap.

Later, I decided not to tell Jack about it. I was afraid he would think I had bought it out of an unrealistic desire to pretend we lived in the forest, not the city. He seemed so much more knowledgeable than I. He did not, for instance, fear the spiders that decorated my kitchen walls. They were as big as my hands, but to him they were harmless, gentle. When I asked about the best way to remove the tree frogs that had moved into the shower stall, he warned they were good luck (I eventually asked the neighborhood children in for Cokes; when they finished, I ordered them to catch the frogs inside their empty glasses.) The salamanders running out from behind my paintings were helpful. The birds which flew in the house unexpectedly through the unscreened windows were normal, like flies. Best of all, they always managed to find a way out.

Sometimes, before getting out of bed in the middle of the night to use the bathroom, I would notice the dark body of a cockroach on the net above me. I never turned on the light to chase the cockroach to a harder surface where I could squash it. I felt a little sorry for the creature, for the net was the sort of shelter that softened the world's harshness.

Consequently, on Thanksgiving morning I looked up at the wall right next to my bed through the net and saw a spider devouring a cockroach, I had mixed feelings. I called aloud for Jack. He had gone to Georgia for the holiday.

I waited for the spider to leave. It was too large to kill. The fan might move it, the mosquito net would protect me, but Jack was the only person I trusted enough to come into the room and shoo it away for good.

ADRIAN CASTRO

*A*drián Castro (1967–) was born in Miami from Cuban and Dominican parents. He writes in the rhythmic Afro-Cuban/Caribbean tradition pioneered by Nicolás Guillén and Luis Pales Matos. He currently lives in Miami Beach where he often performs his poetry with musicians as well as by himself. He has performed around the country in places like The Nuyorican Poets Café in New York, The Naropa Institute in Boulder, Colorado, The Hemingway Literary Festival in Chicago, and the Miami Book Fair International.

He has been published nationally in *Bilingual Review, Paper Dance: 55 Latino Poets, Little Havana Blues, The Miami Herald, Bombay Gin, The New Censorship*, and in Mexico. He has been featured on WLRN's "A Writer's Place," "Cover to Cover," "Rhythm and Roots," and "Topical Currents," and has served as commentator on NPR's "Crossroads." He is also a third of the "Bicycle Poets," a group of poets who regularly bicycle to public schools in Miami and present poetry to kids. Currently, Castro is translating selected works of Luis Pales Matos.

TO RUMBA PLAYERS
OF BELEN, CUBA

. . . an interpretation of a song . . .

*T*hose drums are committed
are relics
for & de that space
where rumba had its crib.
Legacy of aboriginal cane cutters
traders in spice
the deathly odor
of salted meats.
Sweat si & yes
that humidity
that humidity ruffled by the sun.

Bongo conga clave
cajón
these are breathing
museums of two cultures
these are the autochthons
of tone
of rhythm
of speech.

That man leaning on a corner
that woman undulating in a river
that child standing at
a crossroad with
a steel crown
they have not forgotten
the echo of the batá
chiseled into cement
sculptures of hooded monks.
Cobblestone roads hot

as July asphalt
bien caliente because today
September 8th
today tumbadoras are fondled
for La Caridad del Cobre
known around Belén
as Oshún.

Those festivals in plazas presided
by the king Chano Pozo
his fingers aflame
slurrin' hymns in Lucumi
Abakua
Lucumi Arara
raspy rum rails.
Negras with long yellow
skirts copper bracelets
dancing a sensual shake
twinkling their eyes
in a heavy African ogle
cooling honeydew drops
with fans of peacock feather.

Chickens & roosters walking their struts
oblivious to their sacred blood.
Church & jungle symbolized
Seville & Ile Ife ritualized.
Those rumberos will not
forget that marriage arranged
on high seas.
A new identity writ
in ominous swells. A new
breed of troubadour.
Esas negras will continue
the snapping sway of hips
the tremble of thighs
to the crisp leather

crackling wood
their union
bonded by fingers aflame
responding to burning tongues.

Amazing the first tún-tún!
Did Chano Pozo inherit
he whose ears were present
at the first drumming?
Astonishing the first callous!
Oye Chano are your hands homesick
when not beating on goatskins?
Sobering the first sting of rum!
There are some
who say they saw
his birth in Belén.
Some say he wore colored collares/
necklaces so his congas
could commune with deities.
Some even say he baptized rumberos
with rum.

Oye Chano Pozo
did you have calluses
the size of coconuts?
Did you
wear collares
when you
breathed your
last sigh?

IVONNE LAMAZARES

*I*vonne Lamazares (1962–) is a poet and fiction writer who was born in Havana. At the age of fourteen, she left the island with her family. After a three-month stay in Spain, she arrived in Miami where she has lived ever since. She has a doctorate from the University of Miami.

Lamazares received a 1994 Florida Arts Council grant for her fiction. Her poems and stories have appeared in *Linden Lane Magazine* and *Blue Mesa Review*. She has also read at Austin Peay State University in Tennessee as part of a visiting Writers Series and at the National Council of Teachers of English Conference in Orlando, Florida.

Lamazares is a Professor of English at Miami-Dade Community College where she teaches writing and Latin American literature. In 1995, she was awarded an Endowned Chair at the College. She is currently working on a novel about the Cuban/Cuban-American experience. She lives in South Miami, Florida, with her husband, the poet Steve Kronen, and their daughter Sophie.

COUSIN SARITA

*A*buela Dolores cleared the obligatory and superfluous potato salad, the *arroz con pollo*, Abuelo's empty beer bottle, and the half-eaten bread pudding swimming in its unbearably sweet syrup. I followed her to the kitchen where, with her stinky cloth, she wiped the white stove and the sink. As Abuelo listened to the Voice of the Americas behind closed windows, Abuela and I spoke of serious matters. I was eleven, so she liked to stress the importance of keeping my feminine reputation spotless. And to illustrate the point, Abuela Dolores related to me the life and adventures of ungrateful, disreputable cousin Sarita.

Sarita got off the ship from Spain, Abuela said, a sunny morning in June 1959. Waiting to meet her, Abuela wore a perfectly starched white blouse full of embroidered flowers, and a luxurious straw hat she had designed herself. When Sarita appeared in the busy Havana port with her fancy luggage, Abuela looked twice at Sarita's shapely figure, her moorish skin and gray eyes from our Galician side of the family. Suddenly, a black bird, (a *toti*) perhaps curious about the fake fruits in Abuela's straw hat, planted itself on her head. As she smacked the bird, Abuela felt a jolt in her stomach which she later realized was a clear omen of things to come.

Strolling to their taxi, Abuela couldn't help but notice that Sarita was a bubbly conversationalist and born flatterer. She could feel her poor old heart jump in place: Sarita her confidante, a partner to embroider with, to join her in the occasional game of canasta, someone to ease her solitude and help her relive her youthful years. Abuela halted her cleaning motion over the sink and uttered a dramatic sigh. "In fifty years of marriage, your Abuelo has never had a brain for anything but business. I was always left to my own devices. So it's no wonder I didn't send Sarita packing when she finally told me the truth."

A few hours after Abuela had become duly enamored of her charge, Sarita confessed she was four months' pregnant and intended to have the baby in Cuba, in Abuela's house. Abuela's blood pressure rose and her cold sweat drove her to ask for smelling salts. She knew Sarita's marriage in Spain had failed; in fact, Sarita had come to Cuba to get a divorce. There had been rumors that a first son had not been her husband's. The husband didn't know about this pregnancy, cried Sarita; her parents didn't know; nobody knew. She swore the child was her husband's and Abuela did not insist. "I thought, a baby is coming and I will get to embroider beautiful diapers and bibs. Look how unselfish I was," Abuela shook her head slightly as she casually inspected the neighbor's yard through the kitchen window.

That November, baby Nico was born. Abuela was convinced his father was a gypsy because of the infant's curly hair and flat nose. "He didn't look like anyone in the family but like an African nomad or one of those Mayan idols in *Selecciones del Reader's Digest.*" Still, Abuela believed Sarita was ready to put her dubious past behind her. Then on December 21, 1959 (Abuela always remembered the date because she had just put the finishing touches on the Christmas tree), the doorbell rang. Outside stood a dark, tall, well-dressed man of thirty-some years. "I'm here to baptize the child," the man introduced himself. Once again, Abuela's blood pressure rose, pounding her temples. The gentleman strode across the living room to greet Sarita who, smiling, informed Abuela that Andres Soito was a Mexican businessman she had met on the ship coming from Spain who had graciously agreed to be the baby's godfather.

"Imagine giving your son to a dark Mexican stranger to baptize," Abuela said, "a man who came to the island I'm sure only looking to have an adventure, an easy affair with a soon-to-be-available divorcee!" He must have been quite angry (Abuela half-smiled as she dried her hands on her apron) when he realized that Sarita was not as "free" as he would have liked, that she couldn't come and go but that she was going to be chaperoned everywhere.

And so it was. Once he discovered he had wasted the trip, the stranger resigned himself. He was, Abuela admitted, courteous and generous, and his Indian features were "not as ugly" as she had first supposed. He stayed long enough to baptize baby Nico and take Sarita (and Abuela of course) strolling by the Capitol Building. Afterward he flew back to Mexico City; no one heard from him again.

Incomprehensibly to Abuela, Sarita went into a long brooding depression and hardly spoke to anyone. "This is when I made my biggest mistake," Abuela confessed. "To cheer her up, I suggested a picnic, and I invited your Abuelo's country nephew Ignacio, recently arrived from Galicia, who had come to work in Cuba for a few months and send money back to his pregnant wife in Rodeiro."

At first, the picnic appeared to be a disaster. The two - Sarita and Ignacio - seemed to violently dislike each other. They sat at different ends of the table and argued all day about Spanish politics. "They let my special sausage empanada go cold. The villains! I'm sure their antipathy was also part of the scheme."

It was a few days later that Sarita asked if she could enroll in some English classes. Abuela was happy to help her prepare for some occupation, since it seemed she was going to have to fend for herself and her child quite soon. "I never suspected a thing. I took care of baby Nico every Tuesday and Thursday evenings as she took the bus to the Center, books in hand." In this part of the story, Abuela pronounced her words slowly, and her small eyes shone.

Sarita practiced her English daily, mouthing before a mirror the words to a Sinatra single about a rubber tree plant. It was not until the end of summer that Abuela, while making one of her famous empanadas, heard some laughter in the back street. As was her custom when she heard noise at a neighbor's house, she dashed to the window to watch. To her surprise, it was Sarita.

"She came out of Antonia's house wearing the red satin dress I had made for her — much too loud for the daytime or any English class. I thought about going to Antonia and raising hell (politely of course) but that stubborn *gallega* would have pretended a mouse ate her tongue. I know her well. She has always been as loose as Sarita." (Abuela gesticulated wildly, without noticing that Antonia, who was still our backstreet neighbor, had come out to the yard with her small daughter.)

Taking matters into her own hands, Abuela hired a private detective, one of my father's drinking buddies. "I got it between my eyebrows that I was not going to be the idiot, taking care of that baby while she went on her whorish outings. I of course told the detective not to spare me any details. So after a few days, he handed me a long list. First, she took Route 18 to the Capitol Building and met none other than, guess! that sweet country bumpkin, her own cousin mind you, Ignacio. They then walked hand in hand all of Monte to Esperanza Avenue. They ate ice cream, hugged each other in the street with no shame. They sat in Cafe del Prado, Sarita dressed like a queen next to the smiling *gallego* farmer wearing his wrinkled guayabera. In the pictures the detective took," Abuela's voice almost quivered, "could you believe, they looked happy?"

"The rest I should not even tell you," she declared. "They'd disappear into a cheap motel and would come out a few hours later with better color in their cheeks. He would wait with her at the bus stop and kiss her passionately right before she stepped up to the bus. All of this right in the middle of the street."

Abuela fanned herself, her face flushed as if she were experiencing something akin to pleasure. "The pictures were fit to put in an album if it had not been all a disgrace, of course," she added quickly, raising her eyebrows at me. Abuela insisted that the poor country fellow had obviously been seduced by the glamour of a beautiful, sophisticated city woman. It was almost understandable, even if shameful. "Instead of sending money to his poor pregnant wife in Rodeiro, he was spending it all on motels, gifts and dinners with a married woman who had a gypsy baby to care for and was, after all, his own blood cousin."

At last Abuela realized she had been the fool. She had trusted Sarita only to be deceived time and again. So she took drastic action by calling Ignacio over to the house, showing him the pictures "in all their glory" and threatening to mail them to his wife. If, she advised him, he wanted to save face, he simply had to tell Sarita he no longer cared for her. He nodded, shamefaced.

For the next week, Sarita seemed to lose her mind. She hardly ate or slept, and she smoked on the patio day and night. She talked only to Antonia, the ignorant *gallega*, and if Abuela tried innocently to ask about her English classes, Sarita hardly issued a reply. After all, Abuela concluded, Sarita was ungrateful.

"I had taken her in, forgiven her all her lies and kept her from sinking further into the mud. It was time for me to ask her to leave," Abuela's lips puckered, as if she had just swallowed a slice of green guava. But Sarita was, surprisingly enough, almost relieved. By then Baby Nico was sixteen months old, and she decided to fly to Puerto Rico. As a Spanish citizen, she could easily leave Cuba.

Ignacio, of course, went back to his wife in Rodeiro. Sarita tried to phone him, knocked on his door repeatedly (Abuela kept the private eye on her tail) but he never saw her again. "This is just to tell you that you can't lose your head to your heart and you can't be too naive. Sarita lived in her own illusions and, see, she wrecked her life." Abuela sank back in her chair. The moral of the story always seemed to leave her exhausted. Her eyes gradually filmed over, as if she felt sorry for something.

I believed Abuela then, and for a few more years, since I still admired her. But that was long before disreputable cousin Sarita, keeping her taste for cousins intact, would marry my father, Abuela's only child, and bear him a son. She would actually come to see Abuela on her deathbed, and become my lifetime friend.

Sarita is old now and hardly recalls the Ignacio affair except to mention the ridiculous private eye whom they kept making faces at and finally shared *mojitos* with at a bar in Old Havana. Much more important for her was the unexpected visit of that "gypsy Mexican" who had accompanied Sarita on the ship from Spain and whom Abuela never suspected to be Nico's father. It is with him that Sarita claims to have spent the best moments of her life. Except for his kind efforts to help her forget the Mexican stranger, cousin Ignacio and her affair with him did not seem all that memorable to her.

She could not imagine why Abuela would remember, or why she would have retold the story to me with such intimate and passionate care.

SANDRA CASTILLO

Sandra Castillo (1962–) is a poet and English professor at Miami-Dade Community College. She was born in Havana and moved to the United States in 1970 when she was eight years old. She has lived in Florida ever since. Her poetry chapbook *Red Letters* was published by Appalachee Press; currently, she is working on a new collection of poems entitled *Last Night in Havana*, inspired by her recent return to Havana after a twenty-five-year absence.

Individual poems have appeared in national magazines and anthologies including *Cool Salsa: Growing up Latino in the US*; *Paper Dance: 55 Latino Poets*; and *Little Havana Blues*. Castillo also co-founded with colleague and poet Ariel Gonzalez the "Butterfly Lightning Series" at Tobacco Road, a jazz bar in Downtown Miami, as a vehicle to promote local writers. She says that for her, "writing is an act of self-disclosure, a form of meditation."

RINCON

*W*e curve along the edge of civilization:
overgrown cane fields, sombreroed men
with saffron skin and machetes
lining the road we share with farm equipment,
tractors, ox carts, and those who dare
to bicycle the island with children
strapped to homemade-wooden seats
with hope for a Sunday paseo
un día cenizo y triste que se sienta
en mi garganta como un licor extraño.

And you, a product of the revolution,
my cousin, my brother, my love,
have learned to live with horror,
con dolor y escases, con tus ojos triste,
and the sixteen hour night you chase
back to Habana in this choleric air
that blows through the open windows
to touch our shoulders and lick our lips.

It has taken me twenty five years
to get here, to feel these sunburned vinyl seats
stick to my tourist skin with the adhesive that is sweat,
to hold your child who jumps over the dampness
settling inside us, this car,
while you, fascinated by speed and geometry,
spiral through this ash-gray Sunday,
the confused impurity of my thoughts
as your son reaches for his toy alligator,
a Florida souvenir.

MEN ON THE MOON

*T*he year Neil Armstrong landed on the moon,
Tía Velia, our Mariner, sent us a picture
of nine year old Norma.
Hair pulled back, Apollo 11 inscribed
on the white of her t-shirt,
she smiled from the shade of a Florida palm tree.
Surrounded by colors, she stood against a peach house,
the green thickness of American grass
and a turquoise sky.
No longer was America just data:
airmail envelopes, shopping carts, stories
about Tío Luis, who Mother said cut
the surface of Lake Okeechobee
with his body, with his gravel truck,
or Primo Luisito who was in jail for the third,
maybe the fourth time; she was cousin Norma.
She was men on the moon.

And I held on to that picture
as real as a recurring dream and imagined myself flying,
scuffing the surface
of Tía Velia's color photographs,
and like Armstrong's Eagle, landing
in a sea of tranquility.

Later that year,
Fina made each one of us two dresses,
while Mother filled out forms, helped us
give away our clothes, our toys,
and kept us from talking about Norma,
and all those who had left before us.

I BROUGHT ABUELO LEOPOLDO BACK FROM THE DEAD AND MOVED HIM TO MIAMI

*T*hough he died when I was barely five,
though I remember him only as a dark,
silent figure in the black and white
background of childhood,
though he walked around the house
each afternoon looking for abstractions
he claimed to have left on the kitchen counter or his dresser,
though he scared me into believing
we live in a world inside our heads,
I brought Abuelo Leopoldo back from the dead,
sat across him at the dinner table,
stared at the blue of his Caribbean eyes,
wished for his outdoor skin,
wished I could relive my childhood as an adult,
wished I could touch his raw hands, his wrinkled fingers,
the texture-feel of peaches,
and I know I carry him with me
in the part of the self that stores
all that we do not understand
until we can take it out
and say "This is me;
this is who I am."

ANTHONY PEREZ

Anthony Pérez (1969–) was born in New York, grew up in Los Angeles as a child, and has lived in Miami since his teens. His ethnic origins include Cuban, Spanish, African, Mayan, and Chinese. He says of himself: "I'm a pedigreed mutt howling doggerels somewhere in the alleys of Strand, Tate, Neruda, and Guillén."

His poems have been published in *Seneca Review*, *Appalachee Quarterly*, and *Borderlands*, among others, and a book review of Chilean poet Jorge Teillier's *Selected Poems in English Translation* in *Organica Quarterly*. In 1992, he was a semi-finalist in the Discovery/The Nation Award for his poetry.

He received his B.A. at the University of Florida, where he earned an M.F.A in creative writing as well. He is currently teaching freshman English at Miami-Dade Community College and British literature at Belén Jesuit Preparatory School.

MIAMI M TRO ZO

August 24, 1992

Of the birds according to their kinds, and of the
animals according to their kinds, of every creeping
thing of the ground according to its kind, two of
every sort shall come in to you, to keep them alive.

—Genesis 6:20

*T*hey could have been pompons, the flamingos
mangled
in a cyclone's web, thirteen
darting
like cabbages of flame. A palette
of parrots
smeared in a cage. And the aviary,
awry,
shed peacocks' fans and lappet feathers
off other
birds, the harmonica of a toucan's bill whistling
the wind.
Amid trunks of palms and of elephants,
a fence
wrestled a sleepy giant panda
pinned to
a nightmare of wires. Chameleons
and mullions
camouflaged in a tumble of nets hurdled
turtles
and mock boulders. The tortoises, steeped
waist-deep
in muck, started slowly, then rolled like warped barrels
(barely

jutting their limbs) down a bruised route
of raised roots
and kiddy swings from the battered Noah's Park.
Blast or spark,
electric tentacles scribbled the night-
that night
too dark, too late for the keepers
to keep
the zoo from a mob of winds. Daybreak,
they raked
the tusks of pipes, the snake-coiled cables,
and hauled
hippos out of the canal like sofas.

IN CHURCH, CARIDAD LIGHTING A PENNY CANDLE FOR HUITO

Little Havana, 1989

*T*his is not for the stab wounds you showed me
on that balcony the first time we met.

This is not for the cigar box you kept under my bed,
flickered with burns, or the spoon tarnished inside.

This is not for my tarot cards, the ones you used to cut tecata.
This is not for the comic books you took with you.

No more does Professor X stare at the ceiling
from your bedside, spirals in his eyes,

nor Darkhawk's crystal ball unveil the stars
of chipped paint in the dark. It's not for the television

left on while you drifted in a tub,
the faucet dripping, timing your orbit.

It's not for the water tinged with urine that you woke in.
This is for the holy water in the stoop you dabbed.

This is for the rain needling the windowpane,
the fruit vendor's home remedies,

the lemons we squeezed into my bathtub,
the Miami River carrying away the orishas' hexes like rinds.

It's for the green explosion of palm trees
below your window, the ones on Eighth Street

with trunks thick enough to hide you and someone's
    shadow.
Behind the windows of Navarro Discount,

the statues of saints saw nothing.
This is for your eyes, closed like a saint's

in a picture in my purse. This is for Lazarus
running after you, Sebastian pierced with syringes,

stray dogs coming to lick your wounds
until your skin glistened.

ANTHONY PEREZ

ON BEHALF OF THE SPANISH CROWN, WE REGRET ANY INCONVENIENCE

["assisted readymade," Commission Report on
Conditions of the Chinese Coolies in Cuba, 1873]

*M*y chest was injured by blows on the plantation,
and I still suffer constantly from the pain

Yes, the breeze in the Cuban countryside does blow quite hard.
We advise that you stay indoors during hurricanes.

The administrator and the overseer constantly dealt me
thrusts with sticks, or kicked me, and I still suffer
from internal bleeding

Baseball and soccer are popular pastimes in Cuba;
we do take them seriously. Please try not to get in the way.

The master directed negroes to hold me down
and dealt me more than 80 blows with a rattan rod,
and inflicted injuries which caused me to vomit blood

The negroes speak a backward tongue.
And did we mention a stomach can't hold too many red beans?

The humidity having induced a disease of the back,
I was allowed no bed and compelled to sleep on the ground

Did you mistake the cot for a screen? Did the breeze frighten you into
blocking the windows? If it's rough on your body,
imagine how well it beats the humidity.

My foot is diseased, the result of wounds caused by chains

Don't rush from clogs to shoes so quickly,
shoestrings can be very tricky things.
They can add weight to your foot as well, if you're not so
  accustomed.

I was decoyed here and wept every day
and to this and to bad treatment
I attribute the disease of my eyes

Did you not have any mirrors in Canton?
Don't be frightened by ours, they are only trying to be truthful.

ACKNOWLEDGMENTS

"In Trying Times," "Sometimes I Plunge," and "To Belkis, When She Paints" from *Legacies* by Heberto Padilla, translated by Alistair Reid and Andrew Hurley. Translation copyright © 1982 by Alistair Reed and Andrew Hurley. Reprinted by permission of Farrar, Straus & Giroux, Inc.

"Mambo # 3" and "Montuno" from *Next Year in Cuba* by Gustavo Pérez-Firmat. Copyright © 1994 by Gustavo Pérez-Firmat. Published by University of Texas Press at Austin. Reprinted here by permission of the author.

"Dancing at the Chelsea" by Dionisio Martínez from *History as a Second Language* is reprinted by permission. Copyright ©1993 by the Ohio State University Press. All rights reserved.

"Cousin Sarita" by Ivonne Lamazares was first appeared in *Blue Mesa Review*, Spring of 1993.

"Frutas" by Ricardo Pau-Llosa was first published in *Kenyon Review*, Vol. 13, No. 3, Summer 1991.

"Dos Ríos," by Ricardo Pau-Llosa first appeared in *Sonora Review*, No. 21, Summer, 1991.

"La Historia me Absolverá" by Ricardo Pau-Llosa was first published by *Planet*, No. 96, Dec 1992/Jan 1993.

"Assimilation," by Ricardo Pau-Llosa first appeared in *Verse*, Vol. 10, No. 1, April 1993.

"Women Don't Die on the Frontlines," "The Silver Platter," and "My Mother's Homeland" in *Women on the Frontlines* by Belkis Cuza Malé, translated by Pamela Carmell. Translation copyright © 1986 by Pamela Carmell, printed by Unicorn Press. Reprinted by permission from the author.

"Paco" in *Kike* by Hilda Perera, translated by Warren Hampton and Hilda Gonzalez S. Copyright © 1992 by Hilda Perera. Reprinted by permission from the author.

ACKNOWLEDGMENTS

Thanks are due to the following translators for allowing us to print their translations in English of the original texts in Spanish.

Felipe Estevez for his translation of Felix Varela's *Letters to Elpidio.*

Pablo Medina for his translation of José Martí's "The New Pines."

María Elena Valdés for her translation of an excerpt by Martín Morúa Delgado.

Suzanne Jill Levine and Mary Caldwell for their translation of Lydia Cabrera's "How the Monkey Stole the Fruit His Labor."

Ramón Bayardo Rancaño for his translations of "The Little Rabbit Ulán" by Enrique Labrador Ruiz and "Shadows on the Beach" by Carlos Victoria.

Alistair Reed and Andrew Hurley for their translations of Heberto Padilla's poems. Permission granted by the publisher Farrar, Straus, & Giroux Inc.

Pamela Carmell for her translations of Belkis Cuza Malé's poems. Permission granted by author.

David Miller for his translations of poems by Juana Borrero, José Manuel Carbonell, Agustín Acosta, Rubén Martinez Villena, Amando Fernández.

Carolina Hospital for her translations of works by Diego Vicente Tejera, Martín Morúa Delgado, Juana Borrero, José Manuel Carbonell, Agustín Acosta, Rubén Martinez Villena, Ana Rosa Núñez, Martha Padilla, Lydia Cabrera, Carlos Montenegro, Pura del Prado, Juana Rosa Pita.

H. R. Hays and Donald Walsh for their translations of Eugenio Florit's poems. Permission granted by author.

José E. Fernández for his translation of Ana Rosa Núñez' poem "Resurrection." Permission granted by author.

Catherine Rodríguez-Nieto for her translations of Angel Cuadra's poems. Permission granted by author.

Warren Hampton and Hilda González S. for their translation of Hilda Perera's *Kiki.* Permission granted by author.

ABOUT THE EDITORS

CAROLINA HOSPITAL is a Cuban-American poet, essayist, and fiction writer residing in Miami where she teaches writing and literature at Miami-Dade Community College. Her prose and poetry have appeared in numerous magazines and newspapers including *Prairie Schooner, The Washington Post, Tropic* of *The Miami Herald, Mid-American Review, Caribbean Writer, Vista, The Americas Review, Rio Grande Review, Hadyn Ferry Review, Appalachee Quarterly, Confrontation, High Plains Review*, as well as the anthologies *Looking for Home: Women Writing About Exile, Paper Dance: 54, Latino Poets, Barrios and Borderlands, Hispanic American Literature*, and *In Other Words: Literature by Latinas in the U.S.* She has also given numerous poetry readings and lectures on the literature of Latinos in the United States. To date, she has published three books, *Cuban American Writers: Los Atrevidos* (Linden Lane Press 1989), *Everyone Will Have to Listen* (Linden Lane Press 1990), a bilingual edition of poetry by Tania Diaz Castro, and the *Instructor's Guide to Norton's New Worlds of Literature*, co-authored with Carlos Medina.

JORGE CANTERA was born in Havana, Cuba, in 1960. He has resided in Florida since 1970. He has a B.A. and a Certificate in Latin-American Studies from the University of Florida. He has lectured in several U.S. cities and abroad discussing Cuban political and economic issues. He has traveled extensively throughout Africa, Europe, and Latin America. In 1988, Cantera coordinated a privately-funded Cuban refuge assistance and resettlement program. In 1990, he published "Youth in Politics" in *Cuban Heritage Magazine*. He has also published several articles on Cuban issues in *Presencía*. Currently, he is working on two projects: one on the history of Cuban aviation and another on the Cuban-African wars.

Here are some other books from Pineapple Press on related topics.

For a complete catalog, write to Pineapple Press, P. O. Box 3899, Sarasota, Florida 34230, or call 1-800-PINEAPL (746-3275).

The Book Lover's Guide to Florida. Kevin McCarthy, Editor. A literary tour of Florida's writers, books, and literary sites, with contributions from Gary Harmon, David Nolan, Richard Adicks, Stuart McIver, and others.

Florida in Poetry: A History of the Imagination. Jane Anderson Jones and Maurice O'Sullivan, Editors. A comprehensive anthology of Florida poetry from the sixteenth century to the present, including Bartolomé de Flores, Walt Whitman, Langston Hughes, Elizabeth Bishop, James Merrill, Enid Shomer, and Ricardo Pau-Llosa, among many others.

The Florida Reader: Visions of Paradise. Maurice O'Sullivan and Jack Lane, Editors. An anthology of writings that serves as a historical and literary introduction to Florida. Writers include Ralph Waldo Emerson, Zora Neale Hurston, Zane Grey, Marjorie Kinnan Rawlings, and Harry Crews.

Hemingway's Key West. Stuart McIver. A vivid portrait of Hemingway the writer and Hemingway the macho, hard-drinking sportsman during his decade on our southernmost island, including a two-hour walking tour of Hemingway's favorite haunts.

My Brother, Ernest Hemingway. Leicester Hemingway. First published in 1962, a poignant biography of insight and admiration as only a younger brother could write. Pineapple's 1996 edition contains never-before-published letters and photographs.

Spanish Pathways in Florida: 1492–1992. Ann Henderson and Gary Mormino, Editors. An anthology of essays in both Spanish and English on the influence of the Spanish in Florida from the first explorers to recent immigrants.